CW00801895

We have designed this guide with both foundation and higher candidates i≀

- Foundation material in BLUE.

- Higher material in GREEN.

- Grammar sections in RED, integrated into the main section of the booklet so that you can see how the points that we cover apply to a particular topic.

- A mini-test at regular intervals to enable you to assess how your revision is going.

- A section on exam technique.

- A grammar summary.

  The guide is intended for use with any GCSE specification.

CONSULTANT EDITOR ...

- Gaynor Garton - Teacher of Modern Languages at Ousedale School, Newport Pagnell.

CONTENTS

GRAMMAR CONTENTS

This guide is intended to consolidate what you have learnt throughout your course and to refresh your memory as you approach your exams.

- Use our mini-tests to constantly test yourself ... WITHOUT LOOKING AT THE BOOK!

- Don't just read, learn actively! Talk to yourself in Spanish, record yourself, work with a friend, write things down.

- When you have revised a section, tick the boxes on the contents page. This will help you to see how your revision is progressing.

- Jot down anything which will help you to remember, no matter how trivial.

- Remember that our vocabulary lists don't include everything. Use your dictionary to add to them.

- Remember that if you are entered for different levels in the different skills you will need to use both Foundation and Higher level material.

A WORD ABOUT GRAMMAR

Grammar

To get a good GCSE grade you must have a sound understanding of the rules of Spanish grammar, and be able to apply these rules in your own spoken and written Spanish. Throughout this guide we have tried to show you points of grammar in the context of a particular topic.
Where this has not been possible, grammar points have been included in the grammar summary on pages 82 - 92.

You will need to know the following grammatical terms:

1. <u>Noun</u> – the name of an object or person or place
   eg. La <u>mesa</u>, el <u>padre</u>, el <u>estadio</u>

2. <u>Singular and Plural</u> – a singular noun means there is only one thing or person, a plural noun means there is more than one
   eg. Singular el gato, la casa
        Plural los gato<u>s</u>, las casa<u>s</u>

3. <u>Pronoun</u> – used in Spanish to emphasise who is doing the action of the verb
   eg. Come tortilla.
        <u>Ella</u> come tortilla (<u>ella</u> (she) emphasises who the subject is.)

4. <u>Adjective</u>– a 'describing' word, giving more information about a noun
   eg. Un gato <u>negro</u>, una casa <u>roja</u>

5. <u>Verb</u> – a 'doing' word, indicating the actions of people or things
   eg. <u>Juega</u> al tenis

6. <u>Subject</u> – of a verb is the person or thing 'doing' the verb, this is indicated by the ending of the verb in Spanish
   eg. <u>Juega</u> al tenis

7. <u>Direct Object</u> – of a verb is the person or thing which is having something done to it
   eg. Como <u>una manzana</u> (una manzana is the direct object of the verb)

8. <u>Indirect Object</u> – of a verb usually has 'to' or 'for' in front of it (in Spanish, a)
   eg. Voy a dar este libro <u>a mi hermano</u> ('este libro' is the direct object, and 'mi hermano' the indirect object of the verb 'dar')

9. <u>Infinitive</u> – the form of the verb found in the dictionary meaning 'to do' something'
   eg. comprar (to buy); comer (to eat); vivir (to live)

10. <u>Tense</u> – of a verb tells you when the action takes place – in the past, present or future

11. <u>Adverb</u> – describes a verb, often explains 'how', 'when' or 'where'
    eg. Habla <u>rápidamente</u>

12. <u>Preposition</u> – describes the position of a person or thing
    eg. <u>Al lado del</u> cine

Foundation

0 - cero	18 - dieciocho	51 - cincuenta y uno
1 - uno/a	19 - diecinueve	60 - sesenta
2 - dos	20 - veinte	61 - sesenta y uno
3 - tres	21 - veintiuno	70 - setenta
4 - cuatro	22 - veintidós	71 - setenta y uno
5 - cinco	23 - veintitrés	80 - ochenta
6 - seis	24 - veinticuatro	81 - ochenta y uno
7 - siete	25 - veinticinco	90 - noventa
8 - ocho	26 - veintiséis	91 - noventa y uno
9 - nueve	27 - veintisiete	100 - cien(to)
10 - diez	28 - veintiocho	200 - dos cientos(as)
11 - once	29 - veintinueve	500 - quinientos(as)
12 - doce	30 - treinta	700 - setecientos(as)
13 - trece	31 - treinta y uno	900 - novecientos(as)
14 - catorce	32 - treinta y dos	1.000 - mil
15 - quince	40 - cuarenta	2.000 - dos mil
16 - dieciséis	41 - cuarenta y uno	1.000 000 - un millón
17 - diecisiete	50 - cincuenta	1.000 000 000 - un billón

Remember: <u>uno</u> and <u>cientos</u> agree with the noun they describe.

eg. cien gram<u>os</u>/doscient<u>os</u> gram<u>os</u> (100/200 grammes)

Also uno changes to un before a masculine noun eg. tengo <u>un</u> hermano - I have one brother

1st – primero/a	2nd – segundo/a	3rd – tercero/a	4th – cuarto/a	5th – quinto/a
6th – sexto/a	7th – séptimo/a	8th – octavo/a	9th – noveno/a	10th – décimo/a

After 10th cardinal numbers are used

Vocabulary

Los días de la semana – Days of the week

lunes –	Monday
martes –	Tuesday
miércoles –	Wednesday
jueves –	Thursday
viernes –	Friday
sábado –	Saturday
domingo –	Sunday

Los meses del año – Months of the year

enero –	January	julio –	July
febrero –	February	agosto –	August
marzo –	March	se(p)tiembre –	September
abril –	April	octubre –	October
mayo –	May	noviembre –	November
junio –	June	diciembre –	December

Both the days of the week and the months of the year are written with a small letter in Spanish

el martes – on tuesday   en enero – in January

los martes – on tuesdays   en el mes de enero – in the month of January

Las estaciones – Seasons

el invierno –	Winter
la primavera –	Spring
el verano –	Summer
el otoño –	Autumn
en invierno –	in Winter
en primavera –	in Spring
en verano –	in Summer
en otoño –	in Autumn

Las fechas – The date

el cinco de enero –	5th of January
el dieciséis de agosto –	16th of August
BUT el primero de abril –	1st of April

Foundation

It is useful to know the alphabet in Spanish; you may be required to spell something (usually your name) in the oral exam or to listen to a word being spelt.

as in cat, thay, chay, ay, hay, ee, ka, ellyay, ennay, oh, koo, essay, u, uvay doble, ee griega

A B C CH D E F G H I J K L LL M N Ñ O P Q R S T U V W X Y Z

bay, day, effay, achay, hota, ellay, emmay, enyay, pay, airay, tay, uvay, equis, thayta

Telling The Time

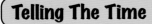

es mediodía – (it is midday)
es medianoche – (it is midnight)

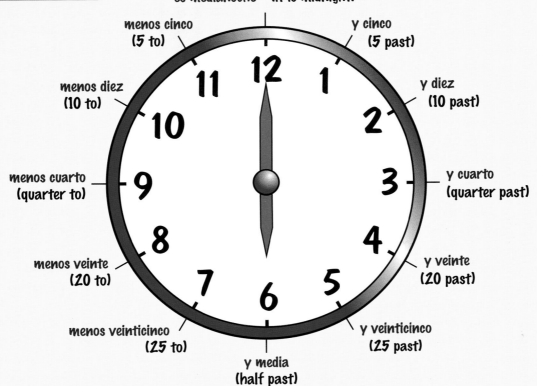

menos cinco (5 to)
y cinco (5 past)
menos diez (10 to)
y diez (10 past)
menos cuarto (quarter to)
y cuarto (quarter past)
menos veinte (20 to)
y veinte (20 past)
menos veinticinco (25 to)
y veinticinco (25 past)
y media (half past)

¿Qué hora es? – What time is it?
Es la una – It is one o' clock.
Son las dos – It is two o'clock.

¿A qué hora...? – At what time...?
Me levanto a las siete – I get up at seven o' clock.

 Remember to use 'es' with times involving one o' clock, and 'son' for all others.

You will also need to be able to understand and use the 24 hour clock.

a.m.		p.m.	
1.00	es la una	13.00	son las trece
3.30	son las tres y media	15.30	son las quince treinta
5.15	son las cinco y cuarto	17.15	son las diecisiete quince
8.45	son las nueve menos cuarto	20.45	son las veinte cuarenta y cinco
10.50	son las once menos diez	22.50	son las veintidós cincuenta

Foundation

¿Cómo eres?
(What do you look like?)
Soy bajo/a y delgado/a.
(I am short and slim.)

¿Cómo te llamas?
(What is your name?)
Me llamo Ana.
(My name is Ana.)

¿Cuál es tu apellido?
(What is your surname?)
Mi apellido es Jones.
(My surname is Jones.)

¿Cuál es tu nacionalidad?
(What nationality are you?)
Soy inglés/inglesa.
(I am English.)

¿Dónde naciste?
(Where were you born?)
Nací en Stafford.
(I was born in Stafford.)

¿Cómo se escribe?
(How do you spell it?)
Se escribe J-O-N-E-S.
(It is spelt J-O-N-E-S.)

¿Cuál es tu número de teléfono?
(What is your telephone number?)
Mi número de teléfono es el 67-94-58.
(sesenta y siete, noventa y cuatro, cincuenta y ocho.)
(My telephone number is 679458.)

¿Cuántos años tienes?
(How old are you?)
Tengo dieciséis años.
(I am 16 years old.)

¿Cuándo es tu cumpleaños?
(When is your birthday?)
Mi cumpleaños es el cinco de enero.
(My birthday is the 5th of January.)

¿Cuál es tu domicilio?
(What is your address?)
Mi domicilio es Calle Church, 20.
(My address is 20 Church Street.)

¿Dónde vives?
(Where do you live?)
Vivo en Cannock.
(I live in Cannock.)

Vocabulary

fecha de nacimiento	date of birth
lugar de nacimiento	place of birth
domicilio	address
estado civil	marital status
soltero/a	single
casado/a	married
separado/a	separated
divorciado/a	divorced
profesión	profession
estudiante	student
escocés/escocesa	Scottish
galés/galesa	Welsh
irlandés/irlandesa	Irish
británico/a	British
la religión	religion
católico/a	Catholic
protestante	Protestant
musulmán/musulmana	Muslim
hindú	Hindu
judío/a	Jewish

alto/a	tall
bajo/a	short
de mediana estatura	medium height
corto/a	short (hair)
largo/a	long
ondulado/a	wavy
rizado/a	curly
liso/a	straight
castaño/a	dark brown
rubio/a	blond
pelirrojo/a	redheaded
guapo/a	goodlooking
feo/a	ugly

(feminine forms shown after '/')

remember
tengo los ojos azules - I have blue eyes
tengo el pelo castaño - I have brown hair

Higher

At Higher level you need to recognise, and also use, language that is more complex and aim for greater accuracy, fluency and variety of vocabulary.

¿Cuántos años tienes?
(How old are you?)
Tengo 15 años de momento pero tendré 16 años la semana que viene.
(I'm 15 at the moment but I'll be 16 next week.)

¿Cuál es tu fecha de nacimiento?
(What is your date of birth?)
Nací el 15 de setiembre de mil novecientos ochenta y cinco.
(I was born on 15th September 1985.)
¿Dónde vives?
(Where do you live?)
Vivo en Bedford desde hace 13 años.
(I've lived in Bedford for 13 years.)
¿Cómo eres de carácter?
(What sort of a person are you?)
Soy simpático/a, inteligente y honesto/a pero me falta paciencia a veces.
(I'm nice, intelligent and honest but I lack patience at times.)

Higher Vocabulary

simpático/a	- nice		extrovertido/a	- outgoing
tímido/a	- shy		agradable	- pleasant
malo/a	- bad		desagradable	- unpleasant
antipático/a	- unfriendly		gracioso/a	- funny
perezoso/a	- lazy		a veces	- sometimes
bueno/a	- good		siempre	- always
trabajador(a)	- hard-working		bastante	- quite
hablador(a)	- talkative		muy	- very
sociable	- sociable		sin embargo	- however

<u>Remember</u>: For feminine forms /a = change 'o' to 'a', (a) = add 'a' to the end of the word.

Grammar TENER AND SER

We will take a closer look at verbs later on. Here are two important verbs which you will use a lot when talking about yourself.

<u>TENER - To have</u>

Tengo	-	I have
Tienes	-	you have*
Tiene	-	he/she/it has/you (formal) have*
Tenemos	-	we have
Tenéis	-	you have**
Tienen	-	they/you (formal) have**

<u>SER - To be</u>

Soy	-	I am
Eres	-	you are*
Es	-	he/she/it is/you (formal) are*
Somos	-	we are
Sois	-	you are**
Son	-	they/you (formal) are**

<u>Remember</u>: The ending of the verb in Spanish lets you know who we're talking about as they do not use pronouns as a general rule, therefore it is very important that you get the ending right.
*use for one person only ** use for more than one person.

Mini Test

It is important to check regularly that you have absorbed the vocabulary and phrases from each section. Here are a few tasks for this section:

1. Say as much as you can about yourself in Spanish, without looking at this guide. Record it onto cassette and time yourself.
2. Play back the tape and see if you can correct your own mistakes.
3. Refer back to the guide and add 5 more details.
4. Practise form-filling. Write out the various headings and without reference to the guide, fill in the form.

Foundation

¿Cuántas personas hay en tu familia?
(How many people are there in your family?)
Hay cinco personas en mi familia, mi madre,
mi padre, mi hermano, mi hermana y yo.
(There are five people in my family, my mother,
my father, my brother, my sister and me.)

¿Tienes un animal en casa? ¿Puedes describirlo?
(Do you have a pet? Can you describe it?)
Tengo un gato. Se llama Snowy, es blanco y muy bonito.
(I have a cat. His name is Snowy, he is white and very cute.)

¿Tienes hermanos?
(Have you got any brothers or sisters?)
Sí, tengo un hermano y una hermana.
(Yes, I have one brother and one sister.)
No, soy hijo/a único/a.
(No, I am an only child.)

¿En qué trabaja tu padre/madre?
(What does your father/your mother do?)
Mi padre es profesor y mi madre es peluquera.
(My father is a teacher and my mother is a hairdresser.)

¿Puedes describir a tu hermano/tu hermana?
(Can you describe your brother/sister?)
¿Cómo es tu hermano/tu hermana?
(What is your brother/your sister like?)
Mi hermano es alto, tiene los ojos azules y el pelo rubio.
(My brother is tall, he has blue eyes and blond hair.)
Mi hermana es baja, tiene los ojos verdes y el pelo castaño. Es delgada.
(My sister is short, she has green eyes and brown hair. She is slim.)

Vocabulary

LA FAMILIA	-	THE FAMILY
el padre	-	father
la madre	-	mother
los padres	-	parents
el abuelo	-	grandfather
la abuela	-	grandmother
los abuelos	-	grandparents
el nieto	-	grandson
la nieta	-	granddaughter
los nietos	-	grandchildren
el tío	-	uncle
la tía	-	aunt
el sobrino	-	nephew
la sobrina	-	niece
el primo	-	cousin(m)
la prima	-	cousin(f)
el niño	-	child
el bebé	-	baby

LOS ANIMALES	-	PETS
el perro	-	dog
el gato	-	cat
el caballo	-	horse
el conejo	-	rabbit
el pájaro	-	bird
el hámster	-	hamster
el conejillo de indias	-	guinea pig
el pez de colores	-	goldfish
el ratón	-	mouse
la tortuga	-	tortoise

<u>Remember</u>
No tengo animales. - I haven't got any pets.
Tiene los ojos azules/el pelo rizado/bigote.
- He/She has blue eyes/curly hair/a moustache.
lleva barba/gafas.
- He/She has a beard/wears glasses.

Higher

¿Te llevas bien con tu familia?
(Do you get on well with your family?)
Sí, me llevo muy bien con mi madre porque siempre es justa.
(Yes, I get on very well with my mother because she is always fair.)
¿Y tu hermano/hermana, te llevas bien con él/ella?
(And your brother/sister, do you get on well with him/her?)
Depende, a veces es bastante molesto/a y nos peleamos.
(It depends, sometimes he/she is annoying and we argue.)

¿Cómo es de cáracter tu madre?
(What sort of person is your mother?)
Es graciosa y trabajadora.
(She is funny and hard-working)
Y tu padre, ¿Cómo es?
(And your father what is he like?)
Depende, a veces es hablador y muy simpático pero cuando está cansado está de mal humor.
(It depends, sometimes he is very nice but when he is tired he is in a bad mood.)

¿Te pareces a tu padre/madre?
(Do you look like your father/mother?)
Sí nos parecemos mucho/un poco.
(Yes, we look very/a little alike.)
No, no nos parecemos para nada.
(No, we don't look at all alike.)

Grammar

Adjectives

An adjective is a DESCRIBING word eg. alto, verde, hablador. All adjectives in Spanish must 'agree' with the noun (the object being described), depending on whether the noun is masculine, feminine, singular or plural. The pattern for regular adjectives is as follows:

Masculine	Feminine	Masculine Plural	Feminine Plural
alto	alta	altos	altas
verde	verde	verdes	verdes
hablador	habladora	habladores	habladoras

You will see that there are 3 patterns depending on whether the adjective ends in an 'o', a vowel or a consonant.

Eg. Mi padre tiene los ojos (masculine plural) verdes.
Mi madre es alta (feminine singular)
Mi hermano es hablador (masculine singular)

Adjectives usually go after the noun is Spanish: Eg. Es un hombre simpático (he is a nice man).

Some adjectives can be used before the noun. When this is the case the masculine singular form is shortened, it loses its 'o'.
Eg. bueno - good
Un buen amigo - A good friend(masculine)
Una buena amiga - A good friend(feminine)

The only adjectives that change in this way are the following:

Bueno - Good   Malo - Bad   Primero - First   Tercero - Third   Alguno - Some   Ninguno - None

Grande has two meanings, big (when used after the noun) or great (when used before the noun). If used before the noun it is shortened to 'gran' whether the noun is masculine or feminine.
Eg. Una gran mujer - A great woman.   Una mujer grande - A big woman.

Foundation

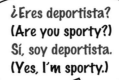

¿Eres deportista?
(Are you sporty?)
Sí, soy deportista.
(Yes, I'm sporty.)

¿Cuándo tocas la guitarra?
(When do you play the guitar?)
En las clases de guitarra del colegio.
(In the guitar lessons at school.)

¿Cuál es tu deporte preferido?
(What is your favourite sport?)
El tenis.
(Tennis.)

¿Tocas algún instrumento?
(Do you play a musical instrument?)
Sí, toco la guitarra.
(Yes, I play the guitar.)

¿Juegas por un equipo?
(Do you play for a team?)
Sí, juego en el equipo del colegio.
(Yes I play for the school.)
No, juego con mis amigos.
(No, I play with my friends.)

¿Por qué te gusta jugar al tenis?
(Why do you like playing tennis?)
Porque es divertido.
(Because it is fun.)

¿Dónde juegas al tenis?
(Where do you play tennis?)
Juego en el parque.
(I play in the park.)

¿Cuándo juegas al tenis?
(When do you play tennis?)
Juego los sábados.
(I play on Saturdays.)

¿Juegas a menudo?
(Do you play often?)
Sí, juego una vez por semana.
(Yes, I play once a week.)

Vocabulary

jugar - to play(sport)	el polideportivo - the sports centre
al tenis - tennis	la pista de hielo - the ice rink
al fútbol - football	el club juvenil - the youth club
al críquet - cricket	el parque - the park
al rugby - rugby	el colegio - school
al baloncesto - basketball	la piscina - the swimming pool
al tenis de mesa - table tennis	el cine - the cinema
al voleibol - volleyball	el teatro - the theatre
al ajedrez - chess	solo/a - alone
a las cartas - cards	con mis amigos - with my friends
tocar - to play(instrument)	con un grupo escolar - with a group from school
la guitarra - guitar	en una orquesta - in an orchestra
la flauta - flute	en un equipo - in a team
la flauta dulce - recorder	a menudo - often
la trompeta - trumpet	de vez en cuando - from time to time
la batería - drums	todos los días - every day
el violín - violin	por la mañana - in the morning
el piano - piano	por la tarde - in the afternoon
el estadio - the stadium	por la noche - in the evening

Higher

¿Qué piensas de la pelota vasca?
(What do you think of 'pelota'?)
Pienso que es un deporte típicamente español.
(I think it is a typically Spanish sport.)

¿Puedes explicar lo que es la 'pelota' porque no se juega en Inglaterra?
(Can you explain what 'pelota' is because it isn't played in England?)
Sí, es parecido al squash pero se juega con la mano en lugar de raquetas y hay dos personas en cada equipo.
(Yes, it is similar to squash but you play it with your hand instead of a racquet and there are two players in a team.)
¿Has jugado a la pelota alguna vez?
(Have you ever played 'pelota'?)
Sí, cuando era más joven jugaba en un equipo.
(Yes, when I was younger I used to play in a team.)

¿Desde hace cuánto tiempo juegas al bádminton?
(How long have you been playing badminton?)
Desde hace cinco años, empecé a la edad de diez años.
(For five years, I started at the age of ten.)

¿Crees que es una buena idea hacer algún ejercicio?
(Do you think it is a good idea to do some exercise?)
En mi opinión es muy importante para la salud.
(In my opinion it is very important for your health.)

Grammar

Verbs in the Present Tense

The present tense is used to describe what you are doing at the present moment in time, eg. *I am playing tennis, or what you do routinely eg. I play tennis every day.

Spanish verbs are divided into three main groups:

Those that end in –AR eg. ganar (to win)   Those that end in –ER eg. correr (to run)

Those that end in –IR eg. salir (to go out) – see p15

ganar – to win		correr – to run	
gano	– I win	corro	– I run
ganas	– you win	corres	– you run
gana	– he/she/it wins/you (formal) win	corre	– he/she/it runs/you (formal) run
ganamos	– we win	corremos	– we run
ganáis	– you win	corréis	– you run
ganan	– they/you (formal) win	corren	– they/you (formal) run

It is essential that you get the correct ending for the person you are talking about in Spanish as they do not as a general rule use pronouns. Therefore the verb ending is the only way to tell who you are talking about.

eg. corro mucho y a veces gano. - I run a lot and sometimes I win.

eg. mi hermano corre de vez en cuando pero nunca gana. - My brother runs from time to time but he never wins.

*This can also be translated by using the present continuous tense. See grammar section p85.

Foundation

¿Qué no te gusta hacer?
(What don't you like doing?)
Odio jugar al ajedrez.
(I hate playing chess.)

¿Qué haces por la tarde/el fin de semana?
(What do you do in the evening/at the weekend?)
Por la tarde hago mis deberes y escucho música.
El fin de semana salgo con mis amigos.
(In the evening I do my homework and I listen
to music. At the weekend I go out with my friends.)

¿Qué te gusta hacer durante
tus ratos libres?
(What do you like to do in your
spare time?)
Me gusta jugar con el ordenador
y me encanta la lectura.
(I like to play on the computer
and I love reading.)

¿Vas a menudo al cine?
(Do you often go to the cinema?)
Voy al cine una vez por mes.
(I go to the cinema once a month.)

¿Sales muchas veces con tus amigos?
(Do you often go out with your friends?)
Salgo con mis amigos todas las tardes.
(I go out with my friends every evening.)

¿Adónde vais?
(Where do you go?)
Vamos al club juvenil o a una fiesta.
(We go to the Youth Club or to a party.)

CINEMA

Vocabulary

montar a caballo – to go horse riding	una comedia – a comedy
montar en bicicleta – to go for a bike ride	coleccionar – to collect
hacer natación – to go swimming	leer – to read
nadar – to swim	una novela – a novel
ir de compras – to go shopping	una historia de amor – a love story
patinar – to skate	una revista – a magazine
hacer footing – to go jogging	un periódico – a newspaper
ir de paseo – to go for a walk	la lectura – reading
salir con amigos – to go out with friends	es interesante – it's interesting
ir a una fiesta – to go to a party	divertido/a – fun
ir al cine – to go to the cinema	estupendo/a – great
un concierto – a concert	aburrido/a – boring
una discoteca – a disco	es bueno para la salud – it's good for your health
salir – to go out	en mi opinión – in my opinion
bailar – to dance	pienso que – I think that
escuchar – to listen	creo que – I think that
ver – to watch (television)	me parece que – it seems to me that
un programa – a programme	tengo la impresión de que – I get the impression that
un documental – a documentary	no aguanto – I can't stand
las noticias – the news	no soporto – I can't stand
las telenovelas – 'soaps'	

Higher

¿Qué hiciste el fin de semana pasado?
(What did you do last weekend?)
Fui al cine con mi novio, vimos una película de ciencia-ficción. Fue excelente.
(I went to the cinema with my boyfriend, we saw a science-fiction film. It was excellent.)

¿Qué vas a hacer el fin de semana que viene?
(What are you going to do next weekend?)
Voy a jugar al tenis el sábado, tengo un partido por la tarde y más tarde voy a terminar mis deberes porque vamos a salir el domingo.
(I'm going to play tennis on Saturday, I've got a match in the afternoon and later I'm going to finish my homework because we're going to go out on Sunday.)

Grammar

Regular – ir Verbs in the Present Tense

SALIR
*Salgo – I go out
Sales – you go out
Sale – he/she/it goes out/you (formal) go out

Salimos – we go out
Salís – you go out
Salen – they/you (formal) go out

Note that 'salir' is irregular in the first person plural as it gains a 'g'. However, it is regular in its endings. Two other very important, but also irregular verbs, are HACER (to do) and IR (to go). Both are frequently used when talking about hobbies and interests.

HACER
Hago – I do
Haces – you do
*Hace – he/she/it does/you (formal) do
Hacemos – we do
Hacéis – you do
*Hacen – they/you (formal) do

IR
Voy – I go
Vas – you go
*Va – he/she/it goes/you (formal) go
Vamos – we go
Vais – you go
*Van – they/you (formal) go

Eg. Hace crucigramas de vez en cuando.
(He does crosswords from time to time.)
Eg. Vamos al cine cada semana.
(We go to the cinema every week.)

*Use of Usted/Ustedes

Remember that the polite form for 'you' in Spanish means that you use the 3rd person ending, normally reserved for he/she/it in the singular and they in the plural, with usted (you, singular) or ustedes (you, plural).

Eg.1. ¿Hace usted crucigramas?
(Do you (singular) do crosswords?)

Eg.2. ¿Van ustedes al teatro?
(Do you (plural) go to the theatre?)

Usted can be abbreviated to Vd. And ustedes to Vds.

Mini Test

Talk for two minutes in Spanish about your hobbies and interests. Include details such as where? how often? with whom? and your opinion of each hobby. When you are happy with your speech, record it onto tape.

Foundation

¿Te apetece salir por la tarde?
(Do you feel like going out this afternoon?)
No puedo, estoy ocupado/a.
(I can't, I'm busy).

Buena idea, podemos ir
al cine más tarde si quieres.
(Good idea, we can go to the cinema
later on if you like.)
Sí, ponen la nueva película
de 'James Bond'.
(Yes, they're showing the
new 'James Bond' film.)

¿Estás libre el sábado?
(Are you free on Saturday?)
Sí, no hago nada por la mañana.
(Yes, I'm not doing anything in the morning.)
¿Te gustaría ir de compras?
(Would you like to go shopping?)
Sí. ¿Buscas algo en concreto?
(Yes, are you looking for anything in particular?)

¿Dónde nos vemos?
(Where shall we meet?)
¿Delante del cine?
(In front of the cinema?)

Busco un regalo para mi amiga.
(I'm looking for a present for my friend.)
Qué bien, me encanta comprar regalos.
(How lovely, I love shopping for presents.)

A las nueve. Podemos quedar a las
nueve y media.
(At nine o' clock. We could
meet at half past nine.)
Vale.
(OK)

¿A qué hora quedamos?
(What time shall we meet?)
¿A qué hora abren las tiendas?
(What time do the shops open?)

HOLLYWOOD
MOVIES

Vocabulary

libre	– free
ocupado/a	– busy
quedar	– to meet
verse	– to meet
una cita	– a meeting
junto/a	– together
apetecer	– to feel like
querer	– to want
poder	– to be able to
vale	– ok
buena idea	– good idea
hasta luego	– see you later
hasta pronto	– see you soon
una entrada	– a ticket (for cinema/theatre)
un billete	– a ticket
una película de ciencia-ficción	– a science fiction film
una película de aventuras	– an adventure film

una película de guerra	– a war film
una película de amor	– a love film
una película de terror	– a horror film
una película policíaca	– a detective film
una película de espionaje	– a spy film
una comedia	– a comedy
un dibujo animado	– a cartoon
una obra de teatro	– a play
una sesión	– a showing
una corrida	– a bullfight
invitar	– to invite
una fiesta	– a party
una barbacoa	– a barbecue
lo siento	– I'm sorry
no puedo	– I can't
tengo que	– I've got to
desgraciadamente	– unfortunately
¡qué pena!	– what a shame!
¡qué lástima!	– what a pity!
¿por qué no?	– why not?
de acuerdo	– ok

Higher

¿Salimos juntos la semana que viene?
(Shall we go out together next week?)
Sí. ¿Te gustaría tomar una copa en el bar nuevo?
(Yes. Would you like to go for a drink in the new bar?)
No, preferiría ir al restaurante.
(No, I would prefer to go to a restaurant.)
¿Por qué no vamos al restaurante mexicano?
(Why don't we go to the Mexican restaurant?)

Vale. Yo voy a reservar una mesa y tú puedes apuntarlo en tu agenda.
(OK. I'll reserve a table and you can make a note of it in your diary.)

¿Te viene bien el sábado a las ocho más o menos?
(Is Saturday at about eight o' clock convenient for you?)
No, lo siento pero tengo una cita el sábado.
(No, I'm sorry but I've got an appointment on Saturday.)
¿Qué tal el viernes entonces?
(How about Friday then?)
Sí, eso me viene mejor.
(Yes, that suits me better.)

Está bien, entonces nos vemos a las ocho delante del restaurante. Se llama 'Chiquitos'.
(That's good, let's meet at eight o'clock in front of the restaurant then, it's called 'Chiquitos'.)

Grammar

Subject pronouns

In English we can emphasise or stress what we are saying simply by changing our tone of voice; in Spanish a SUBJECT PRONOUN is required. Remember that in Spanish you rarely use pronouns unless you particularly want to stress <u>who</u> is doing something.

The subject pronouns are:

Yo – I	Usted (Vd.) – you (formal + singular)	Ellos – they (masculine/mixed)
Tú – you (singular)	Nosotros/as - we	Ellas – they (feminine)
Él – he	Vosotros/as - you (plural)	Ustedes (Vds.) – you (plural + formal)
Ella – she		

Eg. <u>Yo</u> voy a reservar una mesa y <u>tú</u> puedes apuntarlo en tu agenda.
I'll reserve a table and <u>you</u> can make a note of it in your diary.

If there is likely to be any ambiguity you may need to use a pronoun eg. to emphasise that a group is all female.

Eg. Ellas van al teatro esta noche.
They (feminine) are going to the theatre tonight.

Mini Test

1. Practise inviting someone out; suggest different venues, times and places to meet.
2. Practise accepting and refusing invitations, always giving a good excuse when you refuse and suggest an alternative venue/time.

Foundation

¿A qué hora te despiertas?
(What time do you wake up?)
Me despierto a las siete y media.
(I wake up at half past seven.)

¿A qué hora te acuestas?
(What time do you go to bed?)
Me acuesto a las diez y media.
(I go to bed at half past ten.)

¿A qué hora te levantas durante la semana/el fin de semana?
(What time do you get up during the week/at the weekend?)
Me levanto a las ocho menos cuarto durante la semana y a las nueve el fin de semana.
(I get up at a quarter to eight during the week and at nine o clock at the weekend.)

¿Qué haces por la tarde?
(What do you do in the evening?)
Hago mis deberes, ceno a las siete y luego veo la televisión.
(I do my homework, I have dinner at seven o' clock and then I watch television.)

¿A qué hora te lavas?
(What time do you have a wash?)
Me lavo/me ducho a las ocho menos diez.
(I have a wash/a shower at ten to eight.)

¿A qué hora vuelves a casa?
(What time do you get home?)
Vuelvo a casa a las cuatro y cuarto.
(I get home at a quarter past four.)

¿A qué hora te vistes?
(What time do you get dressed?)
Me visto a las ocho.
(I get dressed at eight o' clock.)

¿A qué hora sales de casa?
(What time do you leave the house?)
Salgo de casa a las ocho y veinte.
(I leave the house at twenty past eight.)

¿A qué hora desayunas?
(What time do you have breakfast?)
Desayuno a las ocho y diez.
(I have breakfast at ten past eight.)

Vocabulary

despertarse – to wake up
levantarse – to get up
lavarse – to have a wash
ducharse – to have a shower
vestirse – to get dressed
afeitarse – to shave
peinarse – to brush your hair
lavarse los dientes – to clean your teeth
desnudarse – to get undressed

acostarse – to go to bed
dormir – to sleep
dormirse – to fall asleep
temprano – early
la madrugada – early morning
tarde – late
en primer lugar – first of all
después (de) – after
entonces – then
luego – then
antes (de) – before
finalmente – finally
por último – finally
más – more
menos – less
más o menos – more or less

Higher

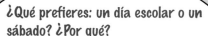

Habla de tu rutina diaria.
(Talk about your daily routine.)
Normalmente me levanto temprano, me ducho y luego me visto...
(Normally I get up early, I have a shower and then I get dressed...)

¿Qué prefieres: un día escolar o un sábado? ¿Por qué?
(Which do you prefer a school day or a Saturday? Why?)
Prefiero el fin de semana porque es más relajado.
(I prefer the weekend because it is more relaxed.)

Y ayer. ¿A qué hora te levantaste?
(And yesterday, what time did you get up?)
Ayer me levanté a las siete.
(I got up at seven o'clock yesterday.)

¿Te acostaste tarde ayer por la noche?
(Did you go to bed late last night?)
No, no me acosté tarde.
(No, I didn't go to bed late.)

Y mañana. ¿A qué hora te levantarás?
(And tomorrow, what time will you get up?)
Me levantaré a las ocho.
(I will get up at eight o' clock.)

Y el fin de semana.
¿Tienes la misma rutina?
(And at the weekend, do you have the same routine?)
Pues, me levanto más tarde y trabajo menos.
(Well, I get up later and I work less.)

Grammar

Reflexive Verbs
The topic 'Daily Routine' contains a number of common REFLEXIVE VERBS:
levantarse (to get up), lavarse (to have a wash), vestirse (to get dressed), acostarse (to go to bed).
'SE' attached to the end of the verb indicates that the verb is reflexive,
i.e. something you do to or for yourself
(lavarse – to wash oneself, as opposed to lavar – to wash something else eg. lavar el coche – to wash the car).
'SE' will move to in front of the verb and will change to agree with the subject of the verb as follows:
Levantarse (to get (oneself) up)

me levanto – I get up	nos levantamos – we get up
te levantas – you get up	os levantáis – you get up
se levanta – he/she gets up	se levantan – they get up

Note that to make the sentence negative you just need to put 'no' in front of the verb,
eg. <u>no</u> me levanto tarde. – I don't get up late.

Mini Test

1. Say 10 things about your daily routine, make sure you use at least 5 reflexive verbs and a variety of times.
2. Say 10 different things about your weekend routine.

Foundation

¿Vives en una casa o en un piso?
(Do you live in a house or a flat?)
Vivo en un chalé grande.
(I live in a large detached house.)

¿Puedes describir tu casa?
(Can you describe your house?)
Es moderna y bastante grande.
(It's modern and quite big.)

¿Cuántas habitaciones hay?
(How many rooms are there?)
Hay ocho habitaciones. Cuatro en la planta baja y cuatro arriba.
(There are eight rooms. Four downstairs and four upstairs.)

¿Puedes describir tu dormitorio?
(Can you describe your bedroom?)
Sí, es muy pequeño, tiene solamente una cama y un armario. Está pintado de amarillo y blanco.
(Yes, it's very small, it has only a bed and a wardrobe. It is decorated in yellow and white.)

¿Qué tipo de habitaciones son?
(What rooms are there?)
Hay tres dormitorios y un cuarto de baño arriba y en la planta baja hay una cocina, un comedor, un salón y otro cuarto de baño.
(There are 3 bedrooms and a bathroom upstairs and downstairs there is a kitchen, a dining room, a living room and another bathroom.)

¿Hay un garaje o un jardín?
(Is there a garage or a garden?)
Sí, los dos. Hay dos jardines, uno delante de la casa y otro detrás.
(Yes, both. There are two gardens, one in front of the house and another behind the house.)

Vocabulary

una casa – a house	una cocina - kitchen	una mesa – table
un chalé – detached house	un cuarto	las cortinas – curtains
una casa	de baño – bathroom	una estantería – shelf
adosada – semi-detached	un dormitorio – bedroom	una lámpara – lamp
una granja – farm	una habitación – room	un escritorio – desk
un piso – flat	un servicio – toilet	un cartel – poster
un sótano – basement	un wáter – toilet	en el suelo – on the floor
un desván – attic, loft	una ducha – shower	a la izquierda de – on the left of
un jardín – garden	una trascocina – scullery	a la derecha de – on the right of
un árbol – tree	los muebles – furniture	entre – in between
una flor – flower	una televisión – television	enfrente de – opposite, facing
un césped – lawn	un estéreo – hi-fi system	en medio de – in the middle of
un invernadero – greenhouse	un vídeo – video recorder	debajo de – below
una terraza – patio, terrace	un ordenador – computer	encima de – above
un vestíbulo – hall	una cama – bed	compartir – to share
una puerta – door	un armario – wardrobe	ordenado/a – tidy
una pared – wall	una cómoda – chest of	desordenado/a – untidy
una ventana – window	drawers	
un salón – living room	una alfombra – rug	
un comedor – dining room	una silla – chair	Remember : de + el = del

Higher

¿Cuántos años llevas viviendo en tu casa?
(How long have you been living in your house?)
Llevo cinco años viviendo aquí.
(I have been living here for five years.)

Describe tu casa ideal.
(Describe your ideal house.)
Mi casa ideal *sería grandísima con veinte habitaciones, una piscina y una pista de tenis en el jardín.
(My ideal house would be really big with 20 rooms, a swimming pool and a tennis court in the garden.)

¿Te gusta tu dormitorio?
(Do you like your room.)
Sí, me gusta bastante, me gustan los muebles, pero no me gusta nada el color de las paredes.
(Yes I quite like it, I like the furniture but I don't like the colour of the walls.)

¿Qué cambiarías de tu dormitorio?
(How would you change your bedroom?)
*Cambiaría las cortinas y la moqueta.
(I would change the curtains and the carpet.)

*for notes on the formation and use of the conditional, see page 37.

Grammar

Radical Changing Verbs in the Present Tense

Some verbs change their 'stem' (beginning) in the 1st, 2nd, and 3rd person singular and the 3rd person plural in the present tense, these are called radical changing verbs. Note that the endings are the normal present tense endings.

Some verbs with an 'e' in the stem, eg. pensar change to 'ie' eg. pienso.

Some verbs with a 'u' in the stem, eg. jugar change to 'ue' eg. juego.

Some verbs with a 'o' in the stem, eg. poder change to 'ue' eg. puedo.

Some verbs with an 'e' in the stem eg. pedir change to 'i' eg. pido.

Now look at the whole verb for each of the above:

Juego = I play	Pienso = I think	Puedo = I can	Pido = I ask for
Juegas = you play	Piensas = you think	Puedes = you can	Pides = you ask for
Juega = he/she plays	Piensa = he/she thinks	Puede = he/she can	Pide = he/she asks for
Jugamos = we play	Pensamos = we think	Podemos = we can	Pedimos = we ask for
Jugáis = you play	Pensáis = you think	Podéis = you can	Pedís = you ask for
Juegan = they play	Piensan = they think	Pueden = they can	Piden = they ask for

Notice how the stem does not change in the 1st and 2nd person plural.
Many verbs follow this pattern.

Foundation

¿Ahorras?
(Do you save?)
Sí. Ahorro cinco libras por semana.
(Yes I save £5 a week.)

¿Te dan dinero tu padres?
(Do your parents give you
pocket money?)
¿Cuánto?
(How much?)
Me dan cinco libras por semana.
(They give me £5 a week.)

¿En qué gastas tu dinero?
(How do you spend your money?)
Compro revistas y ropa.
(I buy magazines and clothes.)

¿Tienes que ayudar en casa?
(Do you have to help with the housework?)
Sí, tengo que fregar los platos y poner la mesa.
(Yes, I have to do the washing up and set the table.)

¿Cuánto ganas?
¿Cuántas horas trabajas?
(How much do you earn? How many
hours do you work?)
Gano veinte libras por día; trabajo
desde las nueve hasta las cinco.
(I earn £20 a day; I work from
9am to 5pm.)

¿Qué haces para ganar dinero? ¿Tienes un trabajo?
(What do you do to earn money?
Do you have a job?)
Cuido a mi hermano de vez en cuando y trabajo en
un supermercado los sábados.
(I look after my brother from time to time and I
work in a supermarket on Saturdays.)

Vocabulary

los quehaceres	– chores	planchar	– to iron
las faenas	– chores	ayudar	– to help
fregar los platos	– to do the washing up	el dinero	– money
lavar la ropa	– to do the washing	dar	– to give
hacer la comida	– to do the cooking	ganar	– to earn
hacer las compras	– to do the shopping	recibir	– to receive
hacer mi cama	– to make my bed	gastar	– to spend (money)
ordenar mi dormitorio	– to tidy my room	comprar	– to buy
sacar la basura	– to put the rubbish out	ahorrar	– to save
cortar el césped	– to cut the grass	una libra esterlina	– a pound sterling
limpiar el coche	– to clean the car	por mes	– per month
poner la mesa	– to set the table	por semana	– per week
pasar la aspiradora	– to hoover ®	trabajar	– to work
pasear al perro	– to walk the dog	en una peluquería	– at a hairdresser's
hacer de canguro	– to babysit	en una tienda	– in a shop
barrer el suelo	– to sweep the floor	de cajero/a	– as a cashier
el bricolaje	– diy	repartir periódicos	– to deliver newspapers

Higher

¿Ayudaste a tu madre en casa ayer?
(Did you help your mother around the house yesterday?)

¿Y la semana que viene qué harás con él?
(And next week what will you do with it?)
Depende, quizás compre un disco si veo
algo que me gusta, si no lo ahorraré.
(It depends, maybe I'll buy a CD if I
see something that I like, if not I'll save it.)

Ordené mi dormitorio como siempre y pasé la
aspiradora también.
(I tidied my room as usual and I hoovered.®)

¿Qué hiciste con tu dinero la semana pasada?
(What did you do with your pocket money
last week?)
Ahorré diez libras para mis vacaciones y me compré
una nueva falda en las rebajas.
(I saved £10 for my holidays and I bought myself
a new skirt in the sales.)

¿Piensas que haces más que tus hermanos
o menos?
(Do you think that you do more than your
brothers or less?)
Hacemos cosas distintas, por ejemplo
mi hermano nunca plancha pero yo sí.
(We do different things, for example
my brother never irons but I do.)

Grammar

The Negative

To make a sentence negative in Spanish (i.e. saying that something is <u>not</u> .....) you simply
need to put 'no' in front of the verb.
Eg. <u>No</u> hago la comida. - I do <u>not</u> do the cooking.

Some other negative expressions consist of two parts which go before and after the verb.

No....nada – **nothing**	No.....nadie – **no one, nobody**
No....nunca/jamás – **never**	No....ni....ni – **neither...nor**
No...ninguno – **no, not any, none**	No...tampoco – **not either**

Eg. <u>No</u> hago <u>nada</u> para ayudar en casa. – I do <u>nothing</u> to help around the house.
<u>No</u> hago <u>ni</u> las compras <u>ni</u> la cocina. – I do <u>neither</u> the Shopping <u>nor</u> the cooking.

You can also use these expressions in front of the verb or on their own:
<u>Nunca</u> ayudo. – I <u>never</u> help.
¿Ayudas en casa? <u>Nunca</u>. – Do you help at home? <u>Never</u>.

Mini Test

1. Describe what each person does around the house in a typical day. Make out a rota in Spanish to make it fairer!
2. Make a list in Spanish of what you have spent your money on over the last month.
3. Explain how/from where you get/earn your money.

Foundation

¿Puedes describir un día típico en el colegio?
(Can you describe a typical day at school?)
Empiezo a las nueve y diez, hay un recreo a las once, la comida empieza a la una y luego termino a las tres y media.
(I start at 9.10am., there is a break at 11.00am., lunch starts at 1.00pm., and then I finish at 3.30pm.)

¿Cómo es tu colegio?
(What is your school like?)
Mi colegio es grande y moderno.
(My school is big and modern.)

¿Cuántos alumnos y profesores hay?
(How many pupils and teachers are there?)
Hay mil doscientos alumnos y noventa profesores.
(There are 1,200 pupils and 90 teachers.)

¿Hay alguna asignatura que no te guste?
(Is there a subject that you do not like?)
Odio las matemáticas, son muy aburridas.
(I hate maths, it is very boring.)

¿Cuántas clases hay por día?
(How many lessons are there a day?)
Hay cinco clases por día.
(There are five lessons a day.)

¿Cuál es tu asignatura preferida?
(Which is your favourite subject?)
Prefiero el español porque es útil.
(I prefer Spanish because it is useful.)

¿A qué hora empiezan las clases?
(At what time do lessons begin?)
Empiezan a las nueve y diez.
(They start at 9.10am.)
¿A qué hora terminan?
(At what time do they finish.)
Terminan a las tres y media.
(They finish at 3.30pm.)

¿Tienes muchos deberes?
(Do you have a lot of homework?)
Tengo dos horas cada día más o menos.
(I have about two hours every day.)

¿Qué asignaturas estudias?
(Which subjects do you study?)
Estudio inglés, historia, francés, y seis más.
(I study English, History, French and six more.)

Vocabulary

la escuela	school (in general)	útil	useful
el colegio	school	inútil	useless
el instituto	school (14-18)	divertido/a	fun
una asignatura	a subject	aburrido/a	boring
una clase	lesson	la historia	History
estudiar	to study	la geografía	Geography
aprender	to learn	el francés	French
enseñar	to teach	el inglés	English
el profesor	teacher	el alemán	German
el recreo	break	las ciencias	Sciences
la comida	lunch	la física	Physics
el horario	timetable	la química	Chemistry
los deberes	homework	la biología	Biology
el boletín escolar	school report	la tecnología	Technology
el uniforme escolar	school uniform	la informática	I.T.
fácil	easy	las matemáticas	Maths
difícil	difficult	el dibujo	Art
interesante	interesting	la música	Music
importante	important	la educación física	P.E.

Higher

¿Qué clases tuviste ayer?
(Which lessons did you have yesterday?)
Ayer tuve dos horas de ciencias y luego una hora de inglés
antes de la comida y dos horas de dibujo después de la comida.
(Yesterday I had two hours of Science and then an hour of
English before lunch and two hours of Art
after lunch.)

¿En tu opinión qué es más interesante,
la música o la informática?
(In your opinion which is the most interesting, Music or I.T.?)
La música es más interesante que la informática porque es fácil,
pero la asignatura más importante para mí es el inglés.
(Music is more interesting than I.T. because
it is easy, but the most important
subject for me is English.)

¿Eres bueno en ciencias?
(Are you good at Science?)
Sí, soy bueno en física porque entiendo las matemáticas
pero encuentro la biología más difícil.
(Yes, I'm quite good at Physics because I understand
Maths but I find Biology more difficult.)

¿Piensas que el uniforme escolar es una buena idea?
(Do you think that the school uniform is a good idea?)
Sí, es muy práctico, siempre se sabe lo que hay que llevar
y además me gusta el uniforme que tenemos.
(Yes, it is very practical, you always know what to
put on and also I like the uniform that we have.)

¿Tu colegio tiene buena fama?
(Does your school have a good reputation?)
Sí, los profesores son simpáticos y trabajadores y
tenemos buenos resultados en general.
(Yes, the teachers are nice and hard-working
and we get good results in general.)

Grammar

Comparative and Superlative of Adjectives

If you want to compare two things or say which you think is the best, here's what you need to do in Spanish:

Use either   más interesante que - more interesting than
               menos interesante que - less interesting than
or   tan interesante como - as interesting as

Eg. El francés es tan interesante como el inglés. - French is as interesting as English.

You may need to make adjectives agree:
Eg. La música es más divertida que la historia. - Music is more fun than history.

To say which you think is the best, worst, most interesting, etc. you can use el más, la más, los más or las más:

Eg. Mi colegio es el más interesante. - My school is the most interesting.
    Mis deberes son los más aburridos. - My homework is the most boring.

Again adjectives need to agree if necessary.

As always, one or two adjectives are irregular:

Eg. bueno/a	mejor	el/la mejor	malo/a	peor	el/la peor
good	better	the best	bad	worse	the worst

Eg. Es el mejor profesor del mundo. - He is the best teacher in the world.
    El francés es peor que el español. - French is worse than Spanish.

Foundation

¿Qué vas a hacer el año que viene?
(What are you going to do next year?)
Voy a seguir con mis estudios/voy a buscar un trabajo.
(I'm going to carry on with my studies/I'm going to look for a job.)

¿Qué asignaturas vas a estudiar?
(Which subjects are you going to study?)
Voy a estudiar ciencias, inglés y dibujo.
(I'm going to study Science, English and Art.)

¿En qué te gustaría trabajar?
(What would you like to be?
What job/career would you like?)
Quiero ser profesor/Voy a ser profesor.
(I want to be a teacher/I'm going
to be a teacher.)

Vocabulary

un/a dependiente/a	– shop assistant	un/a carnicero/a	– butcher
un/a peluquero/a	– hairdresser	un/a panadero	– baker
un/a camarero/a	– waiter/waitress	un albañil	– builder
un/a profesor/a	– teacher	un/a electricista	– electrician
un/a mecánico/a	– mechanic	un/a fontanero/a	– plumber
un/a médico/a	– doctor	un/a programador/a	– programmer
un/a dentista	– dentist	un/a técnico/a	– technician
un/a enfermero/a	– nurse	un/a veterinario/a	– vet
un/a abogado/a	– lawyer	un/a carpintero/a	– carpenter
un jefe de cocina	– chef	un/a periodista	– journalist
un/a secretario/a	– secretary	un hombre de negocios	– businessman
un/a cartero/a	– postman/woman	una mujer de negocios	– businesswoman
un/a bombero/a	– fireman/woman	un/a oficinista	– office worker
un policía/una mujer policía	– policeman/woman	un/una contable	– accountant
un/a obrero/a	– factory worker		

 Change "o" to "a" for female version of the job

<u>Remember:</u>

Me gustaría ser contable. – I would like to be an accountant.

Voy a hacerme veterinario. – I am going to be a vet.

Do not use un/una when talking about your own future career or someone else's career:

Mi padre es carnicero. – my father is a butcher.

Higher

¿Qué esperas hacer en el futuro? ¿Tienes planes para el futuro?
(What do you hope to do in the future?/What are your plans for the future?)
Tengo la intención de seguir con mis estudios y después de ir a la universidad. Más tarde voy a trabajar en el extranjero. Espero casarme y tener hijos un día.
(I intend to carry on with my studies and afterwards to go to university. Later I am going to work abroad. I hope to get married and have children one day.)

Grammar

The Future Tense 1

Just as in English, IR + INFINITIVE can be used to express what is going to happen.
In Spanish, however, you also need 'a' before the infinitive.

Voy a dejar el colegio. – I'm going to leave school.
Va a buscar un trabajo. – He is going to look for a job.
Van a ir a la universidad. – They are going to go to university.

The verb IR is written in full on page 15.

The Future Tense 11

The future tense in Spanish is easy to form. You need to add the following endings to the infinitive:

Trabajar<u>é</u> - I shall work
Trabajar<u>ás</u> - you will work
Trabajar<u>á</u> - he/she will work
Trabajar<u>emos</u> - we will work
Trabajar<u>éis</u> - you will work
Trabajar<u>án</u> - they will work

Eg. Terminaré mis estudios. – I shall finish my studies.
Se casará más tarde. – He will get married later.

Expressions of future time:

Esta tarde - this afternoon/evening
Mañana - tomorrow
Pasado mañana - the day after tomorrow
La semana próxima/la semana que viene - next week
El año próximo/el año que viene - next year
En el futuro - in the future

Verbs which are IRREGULAR in the future tense can be found on the next page.

Mini Test

1. Prepare a speech in Spanish about your school. Mention the subjects you do, your opinion of them and describe one of your teachers.
2. Record yourself on tape talking about your future plans. What are your plans for: Next September, In two years time, In ten years time.

Higher

En primer lugar lo que tienes que hacer antes de llegar a la entrevista.
(First of all what you have to do before arriving at the interview).

¿Cómo viajarás?
(How will you get there?)
Iré en taxi.
(I will go by taxi.)

¿Qué harás para prepararte?
(What wil you do to prepare yourself?)
Prepararé las respuestas a las preguntas posibles.
(I will prepare the answers to possible questions.)

¿A qué hora llegarás?
(What time will you arrive?)
Llegaré temprano.
(I will arrive early.)

¿Qué llevarás puesto?
(What will you wear?)
Llevaré un traje/un conjunto.
(I shall wear a suit (male/female.)

 ## Grammar

Irregular Verbs in the Future Tense
Some common verbs are irregular in the Future Tense. The first part of the verb (the stem) changes, but the endings remain the same. Some common irregular future stems are:

Caber	Cabré	Decir	Diré	Haber	Habré
To fit	I shall fit	To say	I shall say	To have	I shall have
Poder	Podré	Querer	Querré	Saber	Sabré
To be able to	I shall be able to	To want	I shall want	To know	I shall know
Salir	Saldré	Tener	Tendré	Valer	Valdrá*
To go out	I shall go out	To have	I shall have	To be worth	It will be worth
Hacer	Haré	Poner	Pondré	Venir	Vendré
To do	I shall do	To put	I shall put	To come	I shall come

*valer is only really used in the third person i.e. it is worth, they are worth.

Do not forget that the Present Tense can be used in Spanish to express a future idea:
Eg. ¿Vamos mañana? – Shall we go tomorrow?

The Future Tense can also be used in Spanish to express assumption, you need to be careful when you are translating in these circumstances.

Eg. Tendrá unos tres hijos. – He must have about 3 children, NOT he will have about three children.

After 'cuando' when there is implication of a future action you need to use the Present Subjunctive (see p90).
Eg. Cuando tenga treinta años. – When I am 30.

Higher

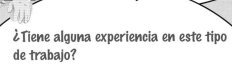

¿Por qué quiere este trabajo?
(Why do you want this job?)
Siempre *he querido trabajar
en una oficina y pienso que
tengo las cualidades y
los títulos necesarios.
(I have always wanted to
work in an office and I think
that I have the necessary
qualities and qualifications.)

¿Qué asignaturas estudió en el colegio?
(Which subjects did you study at school?)
Estudié inglés, matemáticas, ciencias etc.
(I studied English, Maths, Science etc.)

¿Tiene alguna experiencia en este tipo
de trabajo?
(Do you have any experience of this type
of work?)
Sí, trabajo en una tienda los sábados desde
hace dos años.
(Yes, I have been working in a shop on
Saturdays for two years.)
Sí, hice unas prácticas en una oficina
hace cinco meses.
(Yes, I did my work experience in an
office 5 months ago.)

Hábleme un poco de su experiencia laboral.
(Tell me a bit about your work experience.)
Trabajé en una oficina dos semanas. Contesté
el teléfono y fotocopié muchos documentos,
fue bastante interesante.
(I worked in an office for two weeks. I
answered the telephone and I photocopied lots
of documents, it was quite interesting.)

*see p33 for notes on the Perfect Tense

 ## Grammar

The Preterite Tense

There are three past tenses to choose from in Spanish when you want to talk about something
that has happened and is completed and over and done with. It is therefore important that you
choose the correct one. The PRETERITE tense is the equivalent of the Simple Past in English (I did,
I ate etc.) and is used to recount what you did at a particular moment in the past.

Formation:
To form this tense you need to take off the -AR, -ER or -IR from the infinitive and add the endings underlined
below. Note that -ER and -IR verbs have the same endings;

-AR VERBS	- ER VERBS	- IR VERBS
Compré – I bought	Comí – I ate	Viví – I lived
Compraste - you bought	Comiste – you ate	Viviste – you lived
Compró – he/she bought	Comió – he/she ate	Vivió – he/she lived
Compramos – we bought	Comimos – we ate	Vivimos – we lived
Comprasteis – you bought	Comisteis – you ate	Vivisteis – you lived
Compraron - they bought	Comieron – they ate	Vivieron – they lived

Eg. Compré un nuevo traje para mi entrevista. - I bought a new suit for my interview.
   Me preguntó sobre mi experiencia laboral. - He asked me about my work experience.

As always there are some verbs which are irregular in the Preterite Tense, see p87 of the Grammar Summary.

Foundation

¿Vives en una ciudad o en un pueblo?
(Do you live in a town or a village?)
Vivo en el centro de la ciudad/vivo en un pueblo pequeño.
(I live in the town centre/I live in a small village.)

¿Qué hay para los turistas?
(What is there for tourists?)
La catedral es muy bonita y se puede visitar Oxford o Cambridge en tren.
(The cathedral is very pretty and you can visit Oxford or Cambridge by train.)

¿Dónde está Streetly?
(Where is Streetly?)
Streetly está en el centro de Inglaterra a unos diez kilómetros de Birmingham.
(Streetly is in the centre of England about ten kilometres from Birmingham.)

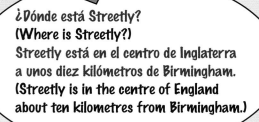

¿Qué hay de interés en Birmingham?
(What is there of interest in Birmingham?)
Hay cines, teatros, y muchísimas tiendas.
(There are cinemas, theatres and lots of shops.)

¿Qué se puede hacer por la tarde?
(What can you do during the afternoon/evening?)
Se puede ir a una discoteca o ir de copas a los bares, también hay muchos restaurantes.
(You can go to a disco or go for a drink in the bars/pubs, there are also lots of restaurants.)

¿Qué se puede hacer durante el día?
(What is there to do during the day?)
Se puede ir de compras, se puede ir a la pista de patinaje o se puede dar un paseo en el parque.
(You can go shopping, you can go to the skating rink or you can go for a walk in the park.)

Vocabulary

una ciudad	a town
un pueblo	a village
en el centro de la ciudad	in the town centre
en las afueras	in the outskirts
en el campo	in the countryside
el barrio	the district/ neighbourhood
la región	the area
estar	to be (location)
cerca de	near to
lejos de	far from
se puede	you can
visitar	to visit
sucio/a	dirty
limpio/a	clean
ruidoso/a	noisy
tranquilo/a	peaceful
aislado/a	isolated
industrial	industrial
congestionado/a	congested
contaminado/a	polluted

precioso/a	lovely
un castillo	a castle
un ayuntamiento	a town hall
un bar	a bar/pub
un restaurante	a restaurant
un museo	a museum
una tienda	a shop
un supermercado	a supermarket
un polideportivo	a sports centre
correos	a post office
un mercado	a market
una iglesia	a church
una catedral	a cathedral
una plaza de toros	a bullring
un banco	a bank
una biblioteca	a library
el norte	north
el este	east
el sur	south
el oeste	west
el noreste	northeast
el centro	centre

Higher

¿Cuáles son las ventajas y las desventajas de vivir en una ciudad/en el campo?
(What are the advantages and disadvantages of living in a town/the countryside?)
En la ciudad hay muchas tiendas y autobuses. Se puede ir al cine y al teatro, pero en cambio hay demasiado tráfico y ruido.
(In town there are lots of shops and buses. You can go to the cinema and to the theatre, but on the other hand, there is too much traffic and noise.)

En el campo puedes estar al aire libre sin coches ni ruido, es pintoresco y se puede pasear. Pero muchas veces no hay nada que hacer y faltan autobuses.
(In the countryside you can be in the open air without cars and noise, it is picturesque and you can go walking. But, often there is nothing to do and there aren't enough buses.)

¿Preferirías* vivir en el campo o en una ciudad? ¿Por qué?
(Would you prefer to live in the countryside or in a town? Why?)
Me gustaría* más vivir en una ciudad porque siempre pasa algo.
(I would prefer to live in a town because there is always something going on.)
Preferiría* vivir en el campo porque me gusta el silencio y la tranquilidad.
(I would prefer to live in the countryside because I like the silence and the tranquility.)

*See p37 for Conditional Tense.

Grammar

Estar
You have already met 'ser' meaning 'to be' on p9, however in Spanish there are two verbs meaning 'to be' depending on the circumstances. <u>ESTAR</u> is used to express geographical location;
Eg. Birmingham <u>está</u> en Inglaterra – Birmingham <u>is</u> in England.
Here is the whole verb;
Estoy – I am
Estás – you are
Está – he/she/it is
Estamos – we are
Estáis – you are
Están – they are
As well as location, ESTAR is also used for temporary states or when a change of state has taken place.
See p57 and 85 for more examples of the differences between Ser and Estar.

Mini Test

1. How many places in a town can you name in one minute? Stop and check vocabulary on the opposite page.

2. Describe your town/village in Spanish, list its facilities, advantages and disadvantages. Record yourself on tape.

Foundation

¿Qué tal el tiempo?
(How was the weather?)
Hizo mucho calor.
(It was very hot.)

¿Adónde vais de vacaciones normalmente?
(Where do you normally go for your holidays?)
Normalmente vamos a la playa.
(Normally we go to the seaside.)

¿Dónde te quedaste?
(Where did you stay?)
Nos quedamos en una pensión.
(We stayed in a guest house.)

¿Cuánto tiempo pasas allí?
(How long do you spend there?)
Pasamos dos semanas con familia.
(We spend two weeks there with family.)

¿Qué hiciste durante las vacaciones?
(What did you do during the holidays?)
Por el día fui a la playa para tomar el sol y nadar en el mar, y por la noche fuimos a los bares.
(During the day I went to the beach to sunbathe and swim in the sea, and at night we went to the bars.)

¿Adónde fuiste de vacaciones el verano pasado?
(Where did you go for your holidays last summer?)
Fui a Grecia una semana con mis amigos.
(I went to Greece with my friends for a week.)

¿Cómo viajaste?
(How did you travel?)
Fuimos en avión desde el aeropuerto de Birmingham.
(We went by plane from Birmingham airport.)

Vocabulary

las vacaciones	– holidays		visitar la región	– to visit the area
veranear	– to spend the summer		el tiempo	– the weather
la Navidad	– Christmas		hace/hacía	– it is/it was
la Semana Santa	– Easter		sol	– sunny
en Francia	– in France		calor	– hot
en Italia	– in Italy		buen tiempo	– nice weather
en Inglaterra	– in England		viento	– windy
en Escocia	– in Scotland		mal tiempo	– bad weather
en el País de Gales	– in Wales		frío	– cold
en España	– in Spain		llueve/llovía	– it is/was raining
en Londres	– in London		nieva/nevaba	– it is/was snowing
en París	– in Paris		está/estaba	– it is/was
en Nueva York	– in New York		nublado	– cloudy
en Edimburgo	– in Edinburgh		despejado	– clear
en el extranjero	– abroad		cubierto	– overcast
en las montañas	– in the mountains		hay/había	– there is/was
la playa	– the beach		una tormenta	– a storm
el mar	– the sea		niebla	– fog
la costa	– the coast		el pronóstico del tiempo	– the weather forecast
tomar el sol	– to sunbathe		cómodo/a	– comfortable
bañarse	– to bathe/swim		lujoso/a	– luxurious
nadar	– to swim		caro/a	– expensive
			barato/a	– cheap

Higher

Háblame de tus vacaciones del año pasado.
(Tell me about your holidays last year.)
Fui a Estados Unidos a esquiar con un amigo. Pasamos dos semanas cerca del lago Tahoe.
Fue excelente, nevó todas las noches pero durante el día hizo sol.
**(I went to the U.S.A. wih my friend to go skiing. We spent two weeks near Lake Tahoe.
It was excellent, it snowed every night but during the day it was sunny.)**

¿Tienes proyectos para este año?
(Do you have any plans for this year?)
Sí, iré a pasar una semana a Francia con amigos y luego pasaré unos días en Barcelona
para visitar los museos de Picasso y Miró.
**(Yes, I'm going to spend a week in France with friends and then I'm going to spend a
few days in Barcelona to visit the Picasso and Miró museums.)**

¿Adónde irías de vacaciones si pudieras elegir?
(Where would you go to on holiday if you could choose?)
Me gustaría ir a la India porque me fascina.
(I would like to go to India because it fascinates me.)

Grammar

The Perfect Tense

The Perfect Tense is used to say what you 'have done' in the past.
It is made up of two parts;

    a) part of 'haber' (used only to help form other tenses)

He – I have	Hemos – we have
Has – you have	Habéis – you have
Ha – he/she/it has	Han – they have

    b) + a past participle (done, bought, eaten etc.) which is formed like this:

        Comprar = compr<u>ado</u>   Comer = com<u>ido</u>
        Vivir = viv<u>ido</u>

You need to remove the –AR, –ER or –IR from the infinitive and add –ADO for –AR verbs and –IDO for –ER
and –IR verbs.

Eg. He viajado en avión – **I have travelled by plane.**
    Hemos visitado el Prado – **We have visited the Prado.**

Some past participles are irregular, see p.**88** of the Grammar Summary.

Mini Test

Record yourself on tape talking about a holiday in the past, and plans for your next holiday.
Pay careful attention to tenses and include as much detail as possible.

Foundation

Por la noche/por la mañana/ In the evening/morning
Buenas noches, que duermas bien.
(Goodnight, sleep well.)
Buenos días. ¿Has dormido bien?
(Good morning. Did you sleep well?)

El Viaje/The Journey
Hola Rebecca, te presento a mi madre.
(Hello Rebecca, let me introduce you to my mother)
Buenos días Señora, mucho gusto.
(Hello, pleased to meet you)
¿Qué tal fue el viaje?
(How was the journey?)
Bien, gracias, un poquito cansado y largo.
(Fine thanks, a bit tiring and long.)

En Casa/At the House
¿Tienes hambre, tienes sed?
(Are you hungry, are you thirsty?)
No, estoy bien, pero estoy muy cansado/a.
(No, I'm fine, but I am very tired.)
Entonces te enseñaré tu dormitorio.
(I'll show you your bedroom then.)

En la mesa/At table
¿Quieres más patatas?
(Do you want some more potatoes?)
Lo siento, no me gustan/sí están riquísimas.
(I'm sorry I don't like them/yes they're delicious.)
¿Puedes pasarme la sal?
(Can you pass me the salt?)

¿Dónde está el cuarto de baño, por favor?
(Where is the bathroom please?)
Está al lado de tu dormitorio.
¿Tienes una toalla?
(It's next to your bedroom. Have you got a towel?)
Sí, tengo una. Gracias.
(Yes, I've got one. Thanks.)

Problemas/Problems
He olvidado mi secador de pelo.
(I've forgotten my hairdryer.)
Te presto el mío.
(I'll lend you mine.)

Vocabulary

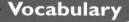

encantado/a	– pleased to meet you
presentarse	– to introduce
tener hambre	– to be hungry
tener sed	– to be thirsty
tener sueño	– to be sleepy
cansado/a	– tired, tiring
¿cómo estás?	– how are you
estoy bien	– I'm fine
así así	– so so
enseñar	– to show
una toalla	– towel
un secador de pelo	– hairdryer

el jábon	– soap
prestar	– to lend
pedir prestado a	– to borrow (from)
servirse	– to help yourself
bienvenido/a	– welcome
estás en tu casa	– make yourself at home
lo siento	– I'm sorry
no sé	– I don't know
no entiendo	– I don't understand
¿cómo se dice...?	– how do you say...?
perdón	– excuse me

Higher

Adiós/Goodbye

Muchísimas gracias señora por su hospitalidad.
Espero volver un día.
**(Thank you very much for your hospitality.
I hope to come back one day.)**
De nada, vuelve cuando quieras.
**(It was a pleasure, come back
whenever you want to.)**

Bienvenido/a – Welcome

Mamá, aquí está mi amiga por
correspondencia inglesa,
se llama Rachael.
**(Mum, here's my English penfriend,
her name is Rachael.)**
Hola Rachael, bienvenida a España,
estás en tu casa.
**(Hello Rachael, welcome to Spain, make
yourself at home.)**
Gracias Señora. ¿Puedo llamar a
mis padres?
**(Thank you, may I call
my parents?)**

Salir/Going out

¿Qué hacemos hoy Rachael?
(What shall we do today Rachael?)
Me da igual.
(I don't mind.)
¿Te apetece ir a la piscina,
te gusta la natación?
**(Do you fancy going to
the swimming pool? do you
like swimming?)**
Sí, que buena idea. ¿Puedes prestarme
un traje de baño?
**(Yes, what a good idea. Can you lend me
a swimming costume?)**

La Comida/Food

¿Te gusta la comida española
Rachael?
(Do you like Spanish food Rachael?)
Sí, me encanta, sobre todo la paella.
(Yes I love it, especially paella.)
¿Hay algo que no te guste comer?
**(Is there anything that you don't
like eating?)**
Solamente las aceitunas, las odio.
(Only olives, I hate them.)

Grammar

Direct Object Pronouns

This is a grammatical term for words such as 'it' and 'them' that we use to replace nouns.
Compare these two sentences:

¿Tienes el pan? – Sí, tengo el pan. - **Have you got the bread? -Yes I've got the bread.**

¿Tienes el pan? – Sí <u>lo</u> tengo. - **Have you got the bread? - Yes, I've got <u>it</u>.**

Notice the position in Spanish; 'lo', 'la' (it) 'los' and 'las' (them) **AS A PRONOUN** come <u>before</u> the verb.
You also need to make your pronoun agree: lo (masculine), la (feminine) los (masculine plural) and las (feminine plural).

Look at these examples:

¿Tienes la paella? – Sí, la tengo. - **Have you got the paella? – Yes, I've got it.**

¿Tienes las patatas? – Sí, las tengo. - **Have you got the potatoes? – Yes, I've got them.**

Other pronouns you should know are; me, te, nos, and os (me, you, us and you).
These operate in the same way:

Eg.   Te amo – **I love you**   Me ama – **he loves me.**
           Os amamos – **we love you**   Nos aman – **they love us.**

Foundation

¿Tiene usted un plano de la ciudad?
(Do you have a plan of the town?)
Sí, aquí está.
(Yes, here you are.)

¿Hay alguna piscina por aquí?
¿Se puede practicar la natación por aquí?
(Is there a swimming pool around here?
Can you go swimming around here?)
Hay una piscina en la Calle Arturo Soria,
a unos cien metros de aquí.
(There's a swimming pool in Arturo Soria
Street, about 100 metres from here.)

Quiero una lista de restaurantes también.
(I'd like a list of restaurants too.)
Sí, por supuesto.
(Yes, of course.)

¿Tiene un horario de autobuses?
(Do you have a bus timetable?)
Sí, están allí.
(Yes, they're over there.)

¿Y a qué hora cierran?
(And at what time do they close?)
Normalmente cierran a las cinco.
(Normally they close at 5 o'clock.)

SRG
Bus
Timetable

¿Los museos están abiertos todos los días?
(Are the museums open every day?)
Todos los días salvo los martes.
(Every day except Tuesdays.)

¿Puede darme alguna información
sobre los monumentos y los museos?
(Can you give me some information
about the monuments and the museums?)
Sí, aquí hay unos folletos sobre los
lugares de interés de aquí.
(Yes, here are some leaflets about
places of interest around here.)

¿Hay excursiones en autocar?
(Are there any coach trips?)
Sí, hay una excursión a Madrid el lunes.
Sale de la Plaza Mayor a las nueve.
(Yes, there's a trip to Madrid on
Monday. It leaves from the
main square at 9 o' clock.)

¿Cuánto cuesta?
(How much does it cost?)
Nada, es gratis.
(Nothing, it's free)

MUSEUM

Vocabulary

una comisaría –	police station
una lista –	list
de hoteles –	of hotels
de campings –	of campsites
de pensiones –	of guest houses
un mapa –	a map
un plano –	a plan
un folleto –	a leaflet
un horario –	a timetable
una excursión (en barco) –	a (boat) trip
abierto –	open
desde –	from
hasta –	to
cerrado –	closed

una oficina de información –	a tourist office
salvo –	except
todos los días –	every day
un día festivo –	bank holiday
gratis –	free
una lista de precios –	a price list
una reducción –	a reduction
un grupo escolar –	a school party
un estudiante –	a student
una entrada –	ticket (to go into a place)
una visita guiada –	a guided visit
alquilar –	to hire
una (tarjeta) postal –	a postcard
un espectáculo –	a show
una feria –	a fair

Higher

¿Sería* posible alquilar bicicletas por un día?
(Would it be possible to hire bicycles for a day?)
Sí, me parece que hay una tienda en el centro
que alquila bicicletas.
**(Yes, I think that there is a shop in the centre
which hires out bikes.)**

Querría* un plano de la ciudad por favor.
(I would like a map of the town please.)
Desde luego, aquí tiene.
(Certainly, here you are.)

Querría* saber si hay una reducción
para grupos escolares.
**(I would like to know if there is a reduction
for school parties?)**
Sí, claro pero tiene que enseñarme un carnet
de identidad.
**(Yes, of course but I need to see
identity cards.)**

Me gustaría* también un mapa de la región
si es posible.
(I would also like a map of the area if possible.)
Lo siento señora, no quedan.
(I am sorry madam, there aren't any left.)

¿Tendría* usted un horario de trenes por si acaso?
(Would you have a train timetable just in case?)
Sí, claro.
(Yes, of course.)

Note that the content here is very similar to
Foundation Level but phrased in a more polite,
sophisticated manner by using the conditional
tense* (see grammar section below).

Grammar

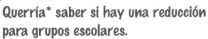

The Conditional Tense

The Conditional Tense is used to translate sentences with 'would' in them. It is easy to
form especially as you have already learnt to form the future tense. All you need to do is to
add the **IMPERFECT ENDINGS** of –ER and –IR verbs to the **INFINITIVE** or **IRREGULAR FUTURE STEM**.

Eg. Visitar<u>ía</u> – I would visit   Visitar<u>íamos</u> – we would visit
     Visitar<u>ías</u> – you would visit   Visitar<u>íais</u> – you would visit
     Visitar<u>ía</u> – he/she/it would visit Visitar<u>ían</u> – they would visit

Note the following useful irregular verbs:

Diría – I would say   Querría – I would like
Haría – I would do   Podría – I would be able to
Pondría – I would put   Vendría – I would come
Sabría – I would know   Saldría – I would go out

Mini Test

1. Using 'querría', ask for 10 different things that you could get from a Tourist Office.
2. Now think of 3 different ways of asking for the same things without using 'querría'.
3. Think of 5 other questions you may need to ask – e.g. prices, times.

Foundation

¿Dónde está el banco, por favor?
(Where is the bank please?)
Siga todo recto y está al final de la calle.
(Go straight on and it's at the end of the street.)

¿Puede ayudarme? ¡Estoy perdido!
No encuentro la comisaría.
(Can you help me? I'm lost. I can't find the police station.)
Baje por la calle y cruce el puente. Está en la plaza mayor.
(Go down the street and cross over the bridge and it's in the main square.)

¿Por dónde se va al ayuntamiento, por favor?
(How do I get to the town hall please?)
Tome la primera a la izquierda y luego la segunda a la derecha.
(Take the first on the left and then the second on the right.)

¿Está lejos la estación de autobuses?
(Is the bus station far?)
No, está a dos minutos a pie, siga todo recto y está enfrente del banco.
(No, it's two minutes on foot, carry straight on and it's opposite the bank.)

¡Perdone usted! ¿Puede decirme dónde está Correos?
(Excuse me, can you tell me where the post office is?)
Cruce la plaza y tuerza a la izquierda y está enfrente de ti.
(Cross the square and turn left and it's in front of you.)

¿Hay una caja de cambio por aquí?
(Is there a bureau de change around here?)
Está muy cerca. Suba por la calle y está a doscientos metros, al lado del cine.
(It's very near. Go up the street and it's about 200 metres away next to the cinema.)

<u>Remember:</u> Expressions followed by 'de' need to change to 'del' when followed by a masculine (el/un) noun.
Eg. enfrente del banco – opposite the bank.
Al lado del cine – next to the cinema.

Also note that you are using 'usted' here as you are asking directions from a stranger, see grammar on page 39 for an explanation of commands using 'usted'.

Vocabulary

siga todo recto	– go straight on	la plaza(mayor)	– the (main) square
está a la derecha	– it's on the right	el río	– the river
está a la izquierda	– it's on the left	la calle	– the road
tome la primera/segunda	– take the first	la carretera	– the main road
/tercera calle	/second/third road	los semáforos	– traffic lights
a la derecha	– on the right	la glorieta	– roundabout
a la izquierda	– on the left	al final de*	– at the end of
cruce	– cross	hasta	– as far as/up to
suba	– go up	al lado de*	– next to
baje	– go down	enfrente de*	– opposite
siga	– follow	detrás de*	– behind
el puente	– the bridge	cerca de*	– near to
		lejos de*	– far from

Higher

¿Para ir a la estación de ferrocarril es mejor ir en autobús o a pie?
(To get to the train station is it better to go by bus or on foot?)
Sería más rápido si coge el autobús.
(It would be quicker if you catch the bus.)

¿Cuál es el mejor camino para ir al mercado por favor?
(Which is the best route to get to the market please?)
Es más fácil seguir las señales, llegará dentro de cinco minutos.
(It is easier to follow the signs, you'll get there within five minutes.)

No he entendido muy bien.
¿Puede repetirlo por favor?
(I didn't understand very well. Can you repeat it please?)
¡Cómo no! Hay que seguir esta autopista....
(No problem, you need to follow this motorway...)

Perdone usted! Estoy perdido.
¿Me puede indicar cómo llegar a Madrid?
(Excuse me, I'm lost. Can you tell me how to get to Madrid?)
Sí, claro, hay que seguir esta autopista hasta el final y llegará sin problema.
(Yes of course, you need to follow this motorway to the end and you'll get there.)

Grammar

Imperatives

Imperatives are instructions or commands.

If you are talking to people that you know i.e. you are using 'tú' or 'vosotros' this is what you need to do:

For 'tú' – use the present tense form and remove the 's';
Trabajas = ¡trabaja! – work!   Comes = ¡come! – eat!   Subes = ¡sube! – go up!

For 'vosotros' – take the infinitive and change the –R to –D;
Trabajar = ¡trabajad! – work!   Comer = ¡comed! – eat!   Subir = ¡subid! – go up!

To form commands for 'usted/ustedes' you need to use the subjunctive
(see grammar summary p90 for an explanation of its uses).

For –AR verbs take the 'I' form of the present tense remove the 'o' and replace it with 'e' or 'en'
Eg. trabajo = trabaje (usted) trabajen (ustedes)

For –ER and –IR verbs take the 'I' form of the present tense remove the 'o' and replace it with 'a' or 'an'
Eg. como = coma (usted) coman (ustedes)   Subo = suba (usted) suban (ustedes)

For notes on negative commands see the grammar summary p86.

Mini Test

Imagine that you are directing a Spanish tourist around your town. Direct him from a hotel to 5 places he may need to go, e.g. bank, post office.

Foundation

En el metro
¡Por favor! Para ir a la Puerta del Sol.
¿Qué línea es?
(Which line is it to get to the Puerta del Sol please?)
Es la línea seis, tiene que tomar la dirección Cuatro Caminos y luego hay que cambiar en Manuel Becerra.
(It's line 6, you have to take direction Cuatro Caminos and then you have to change at Manuel Becerra.)

En el autobús
Quiero ir a la playa. ¿Hay algún autobús?
(I want to go to the beach. Is there a bus?)
Sí, es la línea veinte.
(Yes, it's route 20)

¿A qué hora sale el próximo autobús?
(What time does the next bus leave?)
A las once y cuarto.
(At a quarter past eleven.)

En el tren
¿De qué andén sale el tren para Barcelona?
(From which platform does the train to Barcelona leave?)
Sale del andén tres, vía número dos.
(It leaves from platform 3, track 2.)

¿Cuánto tiempo dura el trayecto?
(How long does the journey last?)
Diez minutos más o menos.
(About ten minutes.)

¿Este autobús para en la playa o tengo que cambiar?
(Does this bus stop at the beach or do I have to change?)
Sí, para en la playa, no hay que cambiar.
(Yes, it stops at the beach, you don't need to change.)

¿Cuánto cuesta un billete de ida para niño y uno de vuelta para adulto?
(How much does a single for a child and a return for an adult cost?)
Dos euros en total.
(2 Euros in total.)

Vocabulary

el barco – boat	bajar – to get off
el aerodeslizador – hovercraft	subir – to get on
el avión – aeroplane	durar – to last
el tren – train	cruzar – to cross
el autobús – bus	el trayecto – journey
el autocar – coach	el viaje – trip
el coche – car	el vuelo – flight
el taxi – taxi	volar – to fly
a pie – on foot	un billete – a ticket
el transporte público – public transport	un bonobús – ticket for 10 trips
viajar – to travel	una ida sólo – a single
una estación – a station	una ida y vuelta – a return
una estación de ferrocarril – railway station	en primera clase – in first class
	en segunda clase – in second class
renfe – Spanish railways	fumador – smoking
una parada de autobús – bus stop	no fumador – non smoking
la llegada – arrival	el puerto – port
llegar – to arrive	el aeropuerto – airport
la salida – departure	le ventanilla – ticket office
salir – to leave/go out	reservar – to reserve

Higher

¿Deberíamos tomar el autobús en lugar del coche?
(Should we travel by bus instead of by car?)
Pienso que deberíamos evitar viajar en coche por el centro de la ciudad por la contaminación, pero será más díficil en el campo.
(I think that we should avoid travelling by car in the town centre because of pollution, but it is more difficult in the countryside.)

¿Has ido a España?
(Have you been to Spain?)
Sí, fui a España el año pasado.
(Yes, I went to Spain last year.)

¿Cómo viajaste?
(How did you travel?)
Fui en avión desde el aeropuerto de Luton porque puedes sacar un billete bastante barato y el viaje es muy corto. Fui al aeropuerto en coche y lo dejé allí.
(I went by plane from Luton airport because you can get a fairly cheap ticket and the journey is very short. I went to the airport by car and left it there.)

¿Cuánto tiempo duró el viaje exactamente?
(How long did the journey last exactly?)
Tardamos cuarenta minutos en llegar al aeropuerto porque no había mucho tráfico y luego el vuelo duró dos horas y media.
(It took us 40 minutes to get to the airport because there wasn't much traffic and then the flight lasted two and a half hours.)

Grammar

Modal Verbs

Certain verbs in Spanish need to be followed by an infinitive, here are three of them:

<u>Poder</u> – <u>to be able to</u>

Puedo – I am able to/can
Puedes – you are able to/can
Puede – he/she/it is able to/can
Podemos – we are able to/can
Podéis – you are able to/can
Pueden – they are able to/can

E.g. Puedo <u>ir</u> en tren – I can go by train.

<u>Saber</u> – <u>to know (how to)</u>

Sé – I know
Sabes – you know
Sabe – he/she/it knows
Sabemos – we know
Sabéis – you know
Saben – they know

E.g. Sé <u>conducir</u> – I know how to drive.

<u>Querer</u> – <u>to want (to)</u>

Quiero – I want
Quieres – you want
Quiere – he/she/it wants
Queremos – we want
Queréis – you want
Quieren – they want

E.g. Quiero <u>ir</u> en barco – I want to go by boat.

Foundation

En la gasolinera/At the petrol station
Llene el depósito, por favor.
(Fill the tank, please.)
Póngame treinta litros de súper, por favor.
(Give me 30 litres of 4 star, please.)

Un accidente/An accident
¡Cuidado!
(Look out!)
Lo siento. ¿Está herido?
(I'm sorry, are you hurt?)
Me duele la pierna.
(My leg hurts)
Voy a llamar a la policía y le daré mi nombre y mi domicilio.
(I'm going to call the police and I'll give you my name and address.)

¿Vende mapas de la región?
(Do you sell maps of the area?)
Sí, y también vendemos refrescos, periódicos y caramelos.
(Yes, and we sell cold drinks, newspapers and sweets too.)

¿Puede mirar el aire de los neumáticos y revisar el agua y el aceite?
(Can you look at the tyre pressure and check the water and the oil?)
He revisado todo, hace falta aceite.
(I have checked everthing, you need some oil.)

Al teléfono/On the telephone
Mi coche tiene una avería, estoy en la N 1 en la carretera de Burgos, a unos veinte kilómetros de Madrid.
(I've broken down, I'm on the N 1 on the road to Burgos about 20 kilometres from Madrid.)
Vale. ¿Qué marca de coche es?
(OK. What make of car is it?)
Es un Seat Ibiza amarillo, la matrícula es GBG 338.
(It's a yellow Seat Ibiza, the registration number is GBG 338.)
¿Puede enviar un mecánico?
(Can you send a mechanic?)
Sí, llegará dentro de quince minutos.
(Yes, he'll be with you in 15 minutes.)

Vocabulary

la gasolina	petrol	el motor	engine
súper	4 star	funcionar	to work
normal	2 star	las luces	lights
sin plomo	lead free	una rueda	wheel
gasoil	diesel	un pinchazo	a puncture
revisar	to check	un taller	a workshop/garage
el aceite	oil	una pieza de recambio	spare part
el agua	water	calentar	to heat
la batería	battery	un ruido	a noise
los neumáticos	tyres	el coche	car
hace falta	it needs	la moto	motorbike
faltar	to lack	el camión	lorry
limpiar	to clean	un herido/a	an injured person
el parabrisas	windscreen	llamar	to call
los frenos	brakes	la policía	police
averiado	broken down	los bomberos	fire service
una avería	a breakdown	una ambulancia	ambulance

Higher

Ha habido un accidente en la carretera NII.
(There has been an accident on the NII.)
¿Qué pasó?
(What happened?)
Un camión iba muy deprisa y chocó con un coche que intentaba salir del parking. El coche frenó pero fue demasiado tarde.
(A lorry was going really quickly and it hit a car which was trying to come out of the car park. The car braked but it was too late.)
¿Hubo algún herido?
(Was anyone injured?)
Creo que sí, el conductor del camión se ha roto el brazo y había mucha sangre.
(I think so, the lorry driver has broken his arm and there was a lot of blood.)

Conducía al centro comercial para ir de compras, no iba deprisa.
(I was driving to the shopping centre to go shopping, I wasn't going fast.)
Estaba subiendo la calle cuando el coche delante de mí se paró sin avisar, frené pero fue demasiado tarde, la culpa no fue mía.
(I was going up the road when the car in front of me stopped without warning, I braked but it was too late, it wasn't my fault.)
No hay muchos daños, solamente algunas abolladuras.
(There's not much damage, just a few dents.)

Higher Level Vocabulary

chocar	–	to bump into	saltarse los semáforos	–	to go through a red light
el permiso de conducir	–	driving licence	desviar	–	to swerve
un cinturón de seguridad	–	seat belt	deslizar	–	to slip/slide
conducir	–	to drive	adelantar	–	to overtake
frenar	–	to brake	la calzada	–	the road
los daños	–	damage	ceder el paso	–	to give way

Grammar

The Imperfect Tense

This is the third of the past tenses that you will be expected to recognise at G.C.S.E. level. It is used to translate the English 'was doing', and to describe actions that went on for some time.

E.g. Conducía lentamente cuando un camión chocó contra mí.

(I was driving along slowly when a lorry crashed into me.)

In the examples given on this page, the Imperfect describes the circumstances before the accident (how things were) and the Perfect Tense is used to describe what suddenly caused the accident.

To form the Imperfect Tense you need to take off the –AR, –ER or –IR and add the following endings:

–AR verbs

Viajaba – I was travelling
Viajabas – you were travelling
Viajaba – he/she/it was travelling

Viajábamos – we were travelling
Viajabais – you were travelling
Viajaban – they were travelling

–ER and –IR verbs

Conducía – I was driving
Conducías – you were driving
Conducía – he/she/it was driving

Conducíamos – we were driving
Conducíais – you were driving
Conducían – they were driving

There are three notable exceptions –ser, ir and ver. See the Grammar Summary p89 for further notes on the Imperfect and these irregular verbs.

Foundation

En la panadería/At the baker's

Buenos días. ¿En qué puedo servirle?
(Good day, how may I help you?)
Quiero dos barras de pan.
(I'd like two loaves of bread.)
Lo siento señora, queda una solamente.
(I'm sorry madam, there is only one left.)
Me la llevo, y cinco panecillos también.
(I'll take it, and 5 bread rolls as well.)
Aquí tiene, tres euros cincuenta en total.
(Here you are, 3 Euros 50 in total.)
Aquí tiene cinco euros.
(Here you are, 5 Euros.)
Aquí tiene un euro cincuenta de cambio señora, adiós.
(Here you are, 1 Euro 50 change madam, good-bye.)

Al mercado/At the market

¿Qué desea?
(What would you like?)
¿Cuánto cuestan las uvas?
(How much are the grapes?)
Dos euros cincuenta el kilo.
(2 Euros 50 a kilo.)

En la tienda de ultramarinos /At the grocer's

¿En qué puedo ayudarle?
(How can I help you?)
Quiero dos botellas de vino tinto, por favor.
(I'd like two bottles of red wine, please.)
¿Algo más?
(Anything else?)
Sí, déme doscientos gramos de aceitunas, por favor.
(Yes, give me 200 grammes of olives, please.)

En la carnicería/At the butcher's

Póngame un kilo de salchichas, por favor
(I'll have a kilo of sausages, please.)
¿Quiere algo más?
(Do you want anything else?)
No, nada más, gracias. ¿Cuánto es?
(No, nothing else thanks. How much is that?)
Son cuatro euros cincuenta.
(That'll be 4 Euros 50.)

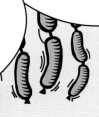

Vocabulary

		el café –	coffee	la lechuga –	lettuce
		el té –	tea	el pepino –	cucumber
una tienda –	shop	el azúcar –	sugar	los tomates –	tomatoes
un mercado –	market	la harina –	flour	los pimientos	
un puesto -	stall	la sal –	salt	rojos –	red peppers
la tienda de		la pimienta –	pepper	las manzanas –	apples
ultramarinos –	grocer's	el chocolate –	chocolate	las naranjas –	oranges
la carnicería –	butcher's	las patatas		las peras –	pears
la panadería –	baker's	fritas –	crisps	los plátanos –	bananas
la pastelería –	cake shop	la mermelada –	jam	las fresas –	strawberries
la bodega –	wine shop	la mantequilla –	butter	las frambuesas –	raspberries
el pan –	bread	las zanahorias –	carrots	las uvas –	grapes
el pastel –	cake	los guisantes –	peas	los melocotones –	peaches
el panecillo –	breadroll	los puerros –	leeks	una sandía –	watermelon
el supermercado –	supermarket	la berza –	cabbage	una piña –	pineapple
el arroz –	rice	las judías verdes –	green beans	un limón –	lemon
la pasta –	pasta	los champiñones –	mushrooms	un pomelo -	grapefruit
las aceitunas –	olives	las cebollas –	onions		
los huevos –	eggs	el ajo –	garlic		
el queso –	cheese	la coliflor –	cauliflower		

Higher

En el mercado/At the market

Buenos días. ¿Qué necesita?
(Hello, what would you like?)

Voy a preparar un gazpacho, así que necesito medio kilo de pimientos rojos, un kilo de tomates, un pepino y un ajo.
(I'm going to make 'gazpacho' so I need half a kilo of red peppers, a kilo of tomatoes, a cucumber and some garlic.)

¿Eso es todo?
(Is that all?)

¡Ay no! Faltan tomates, déme dos kilos de aquellos tomates maduros, parecen buenos.
(Oh no! I haven't got the tomatoes, give me two kilos of those ripe tomatoes, they look nice.)

En la tienda de ultramarinos/At the grocer's

Compré esta leche ayer pero ya se pasó. ¿Puede darme otra?
(I bought this milk yesterday but it has already gone off. Can you give me another one?)

Sí, por supuesto. Esta es muy fresca.
(Yes, of course this one is very fresh.)

Grammar

Gustar, Parecer, Quedar, Sobrar, Faltar and Hacer Falta

These verbs are idiomatic in their usage. You will need to change the order of your sentence and make it the opposite of an English sentence;
E.g. Este pastel me gusta = 'this cake is pleasing to me', however we would translate it as 'I like this cake'.

Because of their nature these verbs are mainly used in the third person (he/she/it/they) – 'gusta', 'gustan'

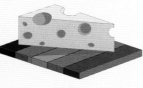

Verb	Literal meaning	Translation
Gustar	To be pleasing	To like, enjoy
Parecer	To seem, to appear	To think (of)
Quedar	To remain	To have (left)
Sobrar	To be left over	To have more than enough/some left over
Faltar	To be missing	To be short of/lack
Hacer falta	To be necessary/needed	To need

Look at these examples;
E.g. Sobran patatas. – There are some potatoes left.
    Lo siento no me queda pan. – I'm sorry, there isn't any bread left.

Mini Test

Write out a shopping list, with quantities, of food needed to prepare your favourite meal (with starter, main course, dessert.)

Foundation

Me gustaría probarme estos zapatos, por favor.
(I'd like to try these shoes on, please.)
¿Qué número calza?
(What size do you take?)

Quisiera ver chaquetas.
(I'd like to see some jackets.)
¿Qué color quiere?
(Which colour would you like?)
Negra, por favor.
(Black, please.)
¿Qué talla gasta usted?
(What size do you take?)
Gasto la talla grande.
(I take a large.)

¿Este suéter es de lana?
(Is this jumper made of wool?)
Sí. ¿Quiere probárselo?
(Yes, do you want to try it on?)
...Me quedo con éste.
(...I'll take this one.)
¿Cuánto le debo?
(How much do I owe you?)
Veinticinco euros.
(25 Euros.)

Tenemos estas chaquetas en gris.
(We've got these jackets in grey.)
¿No las tiene en negro?
(Haven't you got them in black?)
Lo siento, no quedan en negro.
(I'm sorry, there aren't any left in black.)

¿Tiene una talla más grande?
(Have you got a bigger size?)
Lo siento, pero no.
(I'm sorry no.)

¿Puedo probarme esta falda?
(Can I try this skirt on?)
Sí, claro, pase al probador.
(Yes, of course, go through to the changing rooms.)

Vocabulary

un sombrero	hat
una chaqueta	jacket
unos pantalones	trousers
unos vaqueros	jeans
unos pantalones cortos	shorts
una falda	skirt
una camisa	shirt
una camiseta	t-shirt
una blusa	blouse
un vestido	dress
un abrigo	overcoat
un impermeable	raincoat
una corbata	tie
unos guantes	gloves
unas medias	tights
unos calcetines	socks
unos zapatos	shoes
unas sandalias	sandals
unas botas	boots
unas playeras	trainers
una bufanda	scarf
un bolso	bag
un cinturón	belt
un paraguas	umbrella

un probador	changing room
probar(se)	to try on
la marca	make
la talla	size (clothes)
de lana	wool
de algodón	cotton
de seda	silk
de terciopelo	velvet
de nylón	nylon
de tergal/poliéster	polyester
de cuero	leather
el color	colour
blanco/a	white
negro/a	black
rojo/a	red
amarillo/a	yellow
purpúreo/a	purple
marrón	brown
gris	grey
rosa	pink
verde	green
naranja	orange
azul	blue
claro/a	light
oscuro/a	dark

Higher

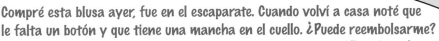

Busco un vestido negro para mi mujer, talla **38**.
(I'm looking for a black dress, size 38, for my wife.)
Tenemos varios, señor, éste es de tergal y ése es de seda.
(We have several sir, this one is made of polyester and this one is made of silk.)
¿Tiene algo más barato? ¿No? ¿Puedo pagar con tarjeta de crédito?
(Do you have anything cheaper? No ? Can I pay by credit card?)
Por supuesto.
(Of course.)

Compré esta blusa ayer, fue en el escaparate. Cuando volví a casa noté que le falta un botón y que tiene una mancha en el cuello. ¿Puede reembolsarme?
(I bought this blouse yesterday, it was in the shop window. When I got home I noticed that it had a button missing and also it has a stain on the collar. Can I have a refund?)
¿Tiene el recibo?
(Have you got the receipt?)
Sí.
(Yes.)
Entonces no hay problema.
(Then there's no problem.)

<u>Remember:</u> Colours are adjectives and must agree with the object they are describing. For information on adjective agreements see page 11.

Grammar

Este, Ese and Aquel

If you want to point out a particular item or person, the different forms of este, ese and aquel are used as follows.

Masculine singular	**Feminine singular**	**Masculine plural**	**Feminine plural**
Este – this	Esta – this	Estos – these	Estas – these
Ese - that	Esa – that	Esos – those	Esas – those
Aquel - that	Aquella - that	Aquellos - those	Aquellas - those

Note that there are two words for 'that'; aquel is used to indicate the one furthest away i.e. that one (over there).

If you want to make these words stand alone to mean 'this one' or 'that one' all you need to do is add an accent;

E.g.   Me gusta el vestido –   ¿éste o ése?
        (I like the dress – this one or that one?)

Do not confuse these words with 'est<u>o</u>', 'es<u>o</u>' and 'aquell<u>o</u>', which are used to refer to an idea or anything which is not specifically mentioned by name.

E.g.   ¿Qué es esto? – **What is this?**

Foundation

En un almacén/In a department store
¿Dónde está la
sección de ropa de señora por favor?
(Where is the women's clothes
department please?)
Está en la tercera planta.
(It's on the third floor.)
¿Y la perfumería?
(And the perfume counter?)
Está en la planta baja, aquí mismo.
(It's on the ground floor, right here.)

Busco un regalo para mi hermana, tiene doce años.
(I'm looking for a present for my sister, she's
12 years old.)
Tenemos estas muñecas, son preciosas.
(We've got these dolls, they're lovely.)

Me hace falta un regalo para mis padres.
¿Qué me recomienda?
(I need a present for my parents, what do you
recommend?)
Estas cerámicas son muy bonitas y a buen
precio, o tenemos carteras de cuero si prefiere.
(These pots are very nice and they're a
reasonable price or we have leather wallets
if you prefer.)
Bueno, pues voy a comprar esta cerámica para
mi madre y una cartera para mi padre. ¿Puede
envolverlas, por favor?
(Right then, I'm going to buy this pot for my
mother and a wallet for my father. Can you
wrap them up please?)

¿Cómo va a pagar?
(How are you going to pay?)
¿Puedo pagar con cheques de viajero?
(Can I pay with travellers cheques?)
Claro.
(Of course.)

Vocabulary

un almacén	a department store	un recuerdo	souvenir
una sección	department	una cinta	cassette
una sección de		un libro	book
ropa de señor	men's clothing section	una muñeca	doll
la perfumería	perfume counter	unos pendientes	earrings
la cosmética	make-up counter	una pulsera	bracelet
la joyería	jewellery section	un collar	necklace
los artículos de viaje	luggage section	un anillo	ring
los artículos de deporte	sports section	un reloj	watch
la planta baja	ground floor	un juguete	toy
la primera planta	first floor	un juego	game
la segunda planta	second floor	un osito	teddy bear
el sótano	basement	un cheque de viajero	travellers' cheque
el ascensor	lift	una tarjeta de crédito	credit card
la escalera mecánica	escalator	buscar	to look for
las rebajas	sales	reembolsar	to refund
un descuento	discount	cambiar	to exchange
envolver	to wrap up	mirar los escaparates	to window shop
un regalo	present		

Higher

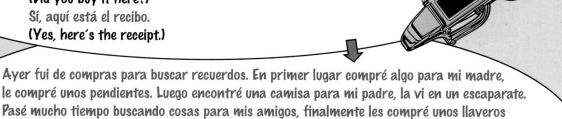

Quiero devolver este reloj. Lo compré ayer y no funciona.
(I want to return this watch. I bought it yesterday and it doesn't work)
¿Lo compró aquí?
(Did you buy it here?)
Sí, aquí está el recibo.
(Yes, here's the receipt.)

Ayer fui de compras para buscar recuerdos. En primer lugar compré algo para mi madre, le compré unos pendientes. Luego encontré una camisa para mi padre, la vi en un escaparate. Pasé mucho tiempo buscando cosas para mis amigos, finalmente les compré unos llaveros porque los coleccionan.
(Yesterday I went shopping to look for souvenirs. First I bought something for my mother, I bought some earrings for her. Then I found a shirt for my father, I saw it in a shop window. I spent a long time looking for things for my friends, finally I bought key-rings for them because they collect them.)

Grammar

Indirect Object Pronouns - to/for me, to/for you, to/for him etc.

Just the same as Direct Object Pronouns (see p35) these come BEFORE the verb
E.g. <u>Le</u> compré una camisa – I bought a shirt for him.

The indirect object pronouns are:
     me – **to me**
     te – **to you**
     le – **to him/her/you (formal)/it**
     nos – **to us**
     os – **to you**
     les – **to them/you (formal)**

They can be attached to the end of a command:
E.g.   Dé<u>me</u> su reloj – **Give (to) me his watch.**
      Dé<u>melo</u> – **give it to me.**
When a direct and indirect object pronoun come together, then the indirect comes first:
E.g.   Voy a reparár<u>selo</u> – **I'm going to repair it for you.**

Note the following changes: le + lo = se lo
                                le + la = se la
                                  le + las = se las
                                  le + los = se los

See grammar summary p91 for more examples.

Mini Test

Write out a shopping list in Spanish of presents, souvenirs and clothes that you would want to buy for various members of your family. Choose a different present for each person and keep to a sensible budget!

Foundation

Quiero enviar este paquete a Francia, por favor.
(I'd like to send this parcel to France, please.)
Hay que pesarlo, costará un euro cincuenta.
(I'll have to weigh it, that'll be 1 Euro 50.)

En el banco/At the bank
En la caja de cambio/At the bureau de change
Buenos días señor, quiero cambiar un cheque de viajero por favor.
(Hello, I'd like to cash a traveller's cheque please.)
Por supuesto. ¿Tiene su carné de identidad?
(Of course, have you got any I.D.?)

Quiero tres sellos de viente centos, por favor.
(I'd like 3 stamps at 20 cents, please.)
¿Puede decirme dónde hay un buzón?
(Can you tell me where the post box is?)
Aquí mismo.
(Right here.)

Sí, aquí está mi pasaporte. ¿A cuánto está la libra esterlina hoy?
(Yes, here's my passport. What is the rate for the pound today?)
Hoy está a un euro treinta y cuatro señor. ¿Cuánto quiere cambiar?
(Today it's at 1 Euro 34 to the pound. How much would you like to change?)

En Correos/At the Post Office
Quisiera mandar una carta y una postal a Inglaterra. ¿Cuánto cuesta?
(I want to send a letter and a postcard to England. How much does it cost?)
Veinticinco centos la carta y veinte centos la postal.
(25 cents for the letter and 20 for the postcard.)

Quisiera cambiar sesenta libras por favor. ¿Hay que pagar comisión?
(I'd like to change 60 please. Do I have to pay commission?)
Sí, el 2%. Firme aquí, por favor.
(Yes, 2%. Sign here, please.)

Vocabulary

el dinero	– money	un formulario	– a form
los billetes	– notes	rellenar	– to fill in
las monedas	– coins	enviar	– to send
un cheque	– cheque	mandar	– to send
un cheque de viajero	– traveller's cheque	pesar	– to weigh
una tarjeta de crédito	– credit card	un paquete	– parcel
cambiar	– to change/cash	una carta	– letter
firmar	– to sign	una tarjeta postal	– postcard
sacar (de)	– to withdraw (from)	un sello	– stamp
la comisión	– commission	un buzón	– post box
el tipo de cambio	– exchange rate	correos	– post office
un pasaporte	– passport	un estanco	– kiosk
un carné de identidad	– identity card		(for stamps/bus tickets)

BANK

Higher

¿Es posible sacar dinero utilizando mi tarjeta de crédito?
(Is it possible to withdraw money using my credit card?)

Sí, por supuesto. ¿Cuánto quiere usted?
(Yes, of course, how much would you like?)

Quiero cuarenta euros; un billete de veinticinco, un billete de diez euros y un billete de cinco euros.
(I'd like 40 Euros; 1 x 25 Euros, 1 x 10 Euros and 1 x 5 Euros.)

¿Si envio esta carta hoy, cuándo llegará a Escocia?
(If I send this letter today, when will it arrive in Scotland?)

Normalmente tarda tres días pero desgraciadamente ahora hay una huelga, así que tardará un poquito más de tiempo.
(Normally, it takes 3 days but unfortunately there is a strike at the moment so it will take a little bit longer.)

Grammar

Por and Para

You will have noticed as you have been working through this book that two words are used to mean 'for' depending on its precise meaning.

Por

Por is used to mean 'through', 'on behalf of', 'by', 'in exchange for', with 'ir' to mean 'to get', with measurements meaning 'per', with parts of the day and with time.

E.g.　Voy <u>por</u> pan <u>por</u> mi madre, voy <u>por</u> la mañana porque hace menos calor. –

I'm going to get some bread for my mother, I'm going in the morning because it's not so hot.

Para

Para is used to express destination or intention, to express purpose or use, in expressions of time to mean 'by' a certain time or for a particular time, with an infinitive to mean 'in order to'.

E.g.　<u>Para</u> coger el tren <u>para</u> Salamanca tienes que estar en la estación <u>para</u> las diez. –

To catch the train for Salamanca you have to be at the station by 10.

Mini Test

1.　You are returning an item recently bought that you are unhappy with. Imagine the conversation.

2.　Imagine yourself at the Bank/Post Office. Think of 5 questions you may need to ask in each place.

3.　Look over numbers (p6) and practise explaining how you would like your money.

Foundation

La Oficina de Objetos Perdidos/ The Lost Property Office

¿Puede ayudarme? He perdido mi reloj.
(Can you help me? I've lost my watch.)
¿Dónde y cuándo?
(Where and when?)
Ayer en la estación de ferrocarril.
(Yesterday at the railway station.)
¿Cómo es?
(What is it like?)
Es de oro con una pulsera de cuero.
(It's gold with a leather strap.)

Alquiler/Hiring

¿Se puede alquilar barcas de pedales aquí?
(Can you hire pedaloes here?)
Sí señor. ¿Cuántas quiere?
(Yes, how many do you want?)
Dos, por favor. ¿Cuánto cuesta por hora?
(Two please, how much does it cost per hour?)
Veinte euros por hora y hay que dejar una fianza de treinta euros.
(20 Euros per hour and you have to leave a deposit of 30 Euros.)

En la Tintorería/At the dry cleaners

¿Hay alguna tintorería por aquí? Mi vestido tiene una mancha y se debe lavar en seco.
(Is there a dry cleaners around here? My dress is stained and it needs to be dry cleaned.)
Hay una en la calle García, tardará un día y costará 20 euros.
(There's one in García Street, it'll take a day and it'll cost 20 Euros.)

Reparaciones/Repairs

¿Me puede reparar esta cámara?
(Can you repair this camera?)
A ver. ¿Qué tiene?
(Let's see. What's wrong with it?)
No funciona. ¿Cuándo estará lista?
(It isn't working, when will it be ready?)
Pasado mañana.
(The day after tomorrow.)

Vocabulary

el aquiler – hiring	encontrar – to find
alquilar – to hire	olvidar – to forget
una bicicleta – bike	robar – to rob/steal
una silla de tijera – deckchair	dejar – to leave
una lancha – motor boat	caerse – to drop
una barca de pedales – pedalo	funcionar – to work
un colchón – lilo	listo/a – ready
una sombrilla – sunshade	una cámara – camera
la tintorería – dry cleaners	las gafas – glasses
lavar en seco – to dry clean	una maleta – suitcase
la joyería – jewellers	un bolso – bag
reparar – to repair	una cartera – wallet
una reparación – repair	contener – to contain
limpiar – to clean	un monedero – purse
revelar – to develop	las llaves – keys
romper – to break	describir – to describe
perder – to lose	la oficina de objetos perdidos – lost property office

Higher

Quisiera alquilar un coche por una semana.
(I'd like to hire a car for a week.)
Puede rellenar este formulario, señor, y tengo que ver su permiso de conducir y su pasaporte también.
(Can you fill in this form, sir, and I need to see your driving licence and your passport also.)
Vale. ¿Cuánto costará por la semana incluído el seguro?
(OK, how much will it cost for the week including the insurance?)

¿Podría reparar estas gafas? Se me cayeron y se ha roto la lente.
(Can you repair these glasses? I dropped them and the lens is broken.)
Sí, sí, podemos repararlas. ¿Podría volver mañana para recogerlas?
(Yes, yes, we can repair them. Can you come back tomorrow to collect them?)

Acabo de llegar y he olvidado el bolso en el taxi. ¿Puede ayudarme?
(I've just arrived and I've left my bag in the taxi. Can you help me?)
Espero que sí. ¿Puede describirlo?
(I hope so. Can you describe it?)
Es bastante grande, de color negro y es de cuero de imitación. Contiene mis llaves, mi pasaporte y mi monedero.
(It is quite big, it's black and it's made of imitation leather. My keys, my passport and my purse are in it.)

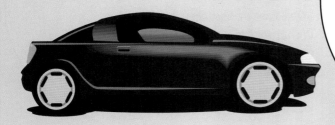

Grammar

Use of 'Se'

Se is often used to avoid using the Passive
('the watch was mended' instead of 'he mended the watch')
it can be translated by 'one' or 'you' or 'we' without meaning anyone in particular. It is often used in notices.

E.g.　Se reparan relojes aquí – watches are repaired here/we repair watches.

E.g.　Se lava en seco ¿no? – It has to be dry cleaned hasn't it?

E.g.　¿Se puede alquilar bicicletas aquí? – Can we/is it possible to hire bikes here.

Mini Test

1. Imagine you have lost your suitcase/handbag at the airport. Describe it and its contents to an official.
2. Make a list of things you must get done before going on holiday.

Foundation

¿Qué sabores hay?
(What flavours are there?)
Tenemos de chocolate, de vainilla, de fresa o de frambuesa.
(We've got chocolate, vanilla, strawberry or raspberry.)
Pues, una bola de vainilla, por favor. ¿Cuánto es?
(Well, a scoop of vanilla, please, how much is it?)

Tengo sed. ¿Quieres beber algo?
(I'm thirsty, do you want a drink?)
Vale, hay un bar allí.
(OK. There's a bar there.)

¿Qué desean ustedes?
(What would you like?)
Para mí un café con leche y para ella una coca cola.®
(For me a white coffee and for her a coca cola.®)

¡Ahora tengo calor! Voy a tomar un helado.
(Now I'm hot! I'm going to have an ice cream.)

¿Quieren comer algo?
(Do you want anything to eat?)
Sí, algo ligero.
(Yes, something light.)

¿Cuánto le debo?
(How much do I owe you?)
Siete euros cincuenta.
(7 Euros 50.)

¿Qué tapas hay?
(What snacks do you have?)
Hay ensaladilla rusa, patatas bravas y bocadillos.
(There is potato salad, roast potatoes with spicy sauce or sandwiches.)
¿Qué clase de bocadillos hay?
(What sort of sandwiches are there?)
Hay bocadillos de queso, jámon y chorizo.
(There are cheese, ham or salami sandwiches.)
Un bocadillo de queso, por favor.
(A cheese sandwich, please.)

Vocabulary

el menú	menu	una tostada	slice of toast
las tapas	snacks/small portions	patatas fritas	chips
una ración	a portion	un perrito caliente	hot dog
un bocadillo	a sandwich	una hamburguesa	hamburger
de queso	with cheese	un café sólo	black coffee
de jamón serrano	with cured ham	un café con leche	white coffee
una tortilla	Spanish omelette (with potato)	un té	tea
		con limón	with lemon
una ensalada	salad	con leche	with milk
calamares	squid	un zumo de naranja	orange juice
queso manchego	cheese	una botella de agua mineral	bottle of mineral water
anchoas	anchovies	con gas	fizzy
champiñones al ajillo	garlic mushrooms	sin gas	still
un helado	an ice cream	una cerveza	beer
de menta	mint	una caña	glass of draught beer
de limón	lemon	una clara	shandy
de fresa	strawberry	un vaso de vino	glass of wine
de frambuesa	raspberry	una limonada	lemonade
		una coca cola®	coca cola®

Higher

¿Dónde quieres ir a comer?
(Where do you want to go to eat?)
No sé, pero un lugar que no cueste mucho, estoy pelado.
(I don't know, but somewhere that doesn't cost much, I'm broke.)

¿Quieres ir al restaurante que vimos el otro día?
(Do you want to go to the restaurant that we saw the other day?)
Prefiero ir a otro sitio donde haya más surtido para los vegetarianos,
y además ése parecía caro.
**(I prefer to go somewhere else where there is more choice for vegetarians,
what's more that one looked expensive.)**

Vale, pues podemos mirar en la guía del ocio y puedes decirme cuál
prefieres, hay una gran variedad.
**(OK, well we can look in the local guide and you can tell me which one you
prefer, there's a wide choice.)**
¿Te apetece ir a la cafetería vegetariana? Mis amigos dicen que vale la pena.
(Do you fancy going to the vegetarian café? My friends say it's worth it.)

¿Qué desean ustedes?
(What would you like?)
Quiero un plato vegetariano que sea bastante ligero, por favor.
(I'd like a vegetarian dish which is quite light, please.)

Grammar

Using QUE, LO QUE, and QUIEN

Used as a linking word 'que' can mean that/which or who.

e.g.
El restaurante <u>que</u> es barato – The restaurant <u>which</u> is cheap.
La chica <u>que</u> trabaja en el restaurante – The girl <u>who</u> works in the restaurant.
Creo <u>que</u> te gustará este plato – I think <u>that</u> you will like this dish.

'Lo que' also has three meanings when used as a linking phrase; what, the thing that and which.

e.g.
<u>Lo que</u> me gusta es la paella – <u>What</u> I like is paella.
La sangría es <u>lo que</u> bebimos en verano – Sangría is <u>what</u> (the thing that) we drink in Summer.

'Quien' is used to mean who or whom. It is only used when referring to a person and replaces 'que' when used after a preposition or when used for emphasis.

e.g.
El camarero con <u>quien</u> hablaba – The waiter with whom I was talking.
Fue mi hermano <u>quien</u> lo hizo – It was my brother who did it.

Mini Test

1. Order snacks, drinks and ice creams for a group of 4 people.

Foundation

La cuenta, por favor.
(The bill, please.)
Gracias señores, el servicio está incluído.
(Thank you gentlemen, the service is included.)

Una mesa para cuatro personas, por favor.
(A table for four, please.)
Sí, señor, al lado de la ventana, ¿Está bien?
(Yes, sir, next to the window, is that alright?)

El menú, por favor.
(The menu, please.)
Aquí tiene, tenemos también un menú del día.
(Here you are, we also have a menu of the day.)

¿Y de postre?
(And for dessert?)
¿Qué son natillas?
(What are 'natillas'?)
Es lo que se llama 'custard' en inglés.
(It's what you call custard in English.)
Natillas para mí entonces.
(Custard for me then.)

¡Camarero! Queremos pedir.
(Waiter! We are ready to order now.)
De primero quisiera una sopa.
(As a starter I shall have the soup.)

¿Y de segundo?
(And as a main course?)
Tráigame un bistec con patatas fritas.
(Bring me steak and chips.)

¿Y para beber?
(And to drink?)
¿Qué nos recomienda?
(What do you recommend?)
El Rioja es muy bueno y muy conocido.
(The Rioja is very good and it is well known.)
Tráiganos una botella de Rioja entonces.
(Bring us a bottle of Rioja then.)
¡Que aproveche!
(Enjoy your meal.)

Vocabulary

el menú	menu	un vaso	a glass
el menú del día	menu of the day	una taza	a cup
entremeses	starters	un plato	a plate/dish
sopas	soups	el camarero/a	the waiter/waitress
verduras y legumbres	vegetables	el cerdo	pork
carnes	meats	el pollo	chicken
aves	poultry	las chuletas	chops
pescados y mariscos	fish and seafood	el cordero	lamb
postres	sweets	la ternera	veal
bebidas	drinks	gambas	prawns
servicio incluído	service included	trucha	trout
una propina	tip	sardinas	sardines
la cuenta	the bill	el bacalao	cod
un plato combinado	set main course	la paella	rice dish with seafood
un tenedor	a fork	la sangría	red wine, lemonade and fruit punch
una cuchara	a spoon	la cava	champagne
un cuchillo	knife		

Higher

La paella es riquísima señora.
(The paella is delicious madam.)
¿Qué es exactamente, qué contiene?
(What is it exactly, what's in it?)
Hay muchas variedades con pollo, mariscos y otras carnes, pero siempre contiene pimentones, tomates y arroz cocido con una pizca de azafrán.
(There are many varieties with chicken, seafood and other meats but it always has paprika, tomatoes and rice cooked with a pinch of saffron.)
¿Le puede hacer sin carne? Es que soy vegetariana y no como ni carne ni pescado.
(Can you make it without meat because I'm a vegetarian and I don't eat meat or fish.)

¿Le gustó el cocido madrileño señora?
(Did you like the stew, madam?)
Lo siento, pero no me gustó el sabor. Estaba muy salado.
(I'm sorry but I didn't like the flavour and it was very salty.)
¿Quién se lo recomendó?
(Who recommended it to you?)
El camarero me dijo que era delicioso.
(the waiter told me that was delicious.)
¿Me permite que le invite a un coñac?
(Can we offer you a brandy on the house then?)
Gracias, pero no bebo alcohol.
(Thank you but I don't drink alcohol.)

Grammar

Ser and Estar
You have met both of these verbs meaning 'to be' on p9 and 31 Now here are a few rules on which one to use when.

Ser
Ser is used to describe permanent states, for example to state your nationality, profession or religion:
E.g.   <u>Soy</u> inglesa, <u>soy</u> profesora y <u>soy</u> católica. – I am English, I'm a teacher and I am Catholic.
It is also used to talk about facts that cannot change;
E.g.   El hielo <u>es</u> frío – Ice is cold.
It is used to describe personality and is used for times, dates and numbers;
E.g.   Mi padre <u>es</u> gracioso – My father is funny.
         ¿Cuánto <u>es</u>? – How much is it?

Estar
Estar is more temporary in nature.
It is used to state position or location;
E.g.   Leeds <u>está</u> en el norte de Inglaterra, <u>está</u> cerca de Wakefield.
         (Leeds is in the north of England, it is near Wakefield.)
It is also used to talk about a condition that may change i.e. usually with an adjective:
E.g.   María <u>está</u> enferma – María is ill.
         Los platos <u>están</u> sucios – The plates are dirty.

Mini Test

List as many items of food and drink as you can in the form of a menu with prices. Now order yourself and your friend a 3 course meal!

Foundation

Quisiera reservar una habitación doble, por favor.
(I would like to reserve a double room, please.)
Sí. ¿A qué nombre?
(Yes, what's the name?)
A nombre de Taylor.
(The name is Taylor.)

¡No hay toallas, la almohada está sucia y el grifo no funciona!
(There aren't any towels, the pillow is dirty and the tap doesn't work!)
No se preocupe usted, arreglaré todo enseguida.
(Don't worry, I'll sort everything out straight away.)

¿Quiere usted una habitación con ducha o con baño?
(Would you like a room with a shower or a bathroom?)
Con baño, por favor y también con balcón.
(With a bathroom please, and also with a balcony.)

¿A qué hora sirven el desayuno?
(What time do they serve breakfast?)
El desayuno es de las siete y media a las diez.
(Breakfast is from 7.30am. until 10.00am.)

hotel

¿Para cuántas noches?
(How many nights is it for?)
Para tres noches.
(For 3 nights.)

¿Va incluído el desayuno en el precio?
(Is breakfast included in the price?)
No señor, hay que pagar un suplemento.
(No sir, you have to pay extra.)

¿Tiene la llave?
(Have you got the key?)
Sí, aquí está, está en el tercer piso, número 312.
(Yes, here it is, it's on the third floor, number 312.)

Vale. ¿Cuánto cuesta?
(OK, how much is it?)
Cuesta quince mil pesetas por noche.
(It costs 15,000 pesetas a night.)

Vocabulary

una habitación – a room	la recepción – reception
doble – double	la llave – key
individual – single	la toalla – towel
libre – free	el grifo – tap
completo – full	el ascensor – lift
una sábana – a sheet	la escalera – stairs
una manta – a blanket	el pasillo – corridor
una almohada – a pillow	una noche – a night
un balcón – a balcony	costar – to cost
con vista del mar – with sea view	inclusive – inclusive
con ducha – with shower	la media pensión – half board
con baño – with bathroom	la pensión completa – full board
un enchufe – a plug	reservar – to reserve
una máquina de afeitar – a shaver	una estrella – a star
una caja fuerte – a safe	una pensión – guest house

Higher

Por teléfono/**On the telephone**
Hotel Rialto, dígame.
(Hotel Rialto, hello.)
Me gustaría saber si quedan habitaciones del 17
al 21 de agosto, por favor.
**(I'd like to know if you have any rooms left for the 17th
to the 21st August, please.)**
Sí señora, tenemos una habitación para esas fechas.
(Yes madam, we have a room for those dates.)
¿Puedo reservarla, por favor?
(Can I reserve it, please.)
Sí, hay que confirmarlo por fax.
(Yes, you need to confirm by fax.)

Quiero hacer una reclamación sobre el estado de mi habitación.
(I'd like to make a complaint about the state of my room.)
¿Qué le pasa señora?
(What's wrong with it madam?)
Pues, en primer lugar no tiene mantas, además la camarera no ha limpiado el baño y lo peor*
es que en la habitación de al lado hicieron muchísimo* ruido anoche.
**(Well, in the first place there are no blankets, also the maid hasn't cleaned the
bathroom and the worse thing is that they made a lot of noise in the room
next door last night.)**

Grammar

Lo + ADJECTIVE AND ADJECTIVES ENDING IN –ísimo

You can use lo + an adjective to express a general idea, it is usually translated in English by the... thing.

e.g. <u>lo bueno</u> es... - <u>the good thing is...</u>   <u>lo malo</u> es... - <u>the bad thing is....</u>
<u>lo importante</u> es que es barato – <u>the important thing/what is important</u> is that it is cheap.

To emphasise adjectives you can add these endings to them:
'-´ísimo', -´ísima', 'ísimos' or 'ísimas' (depending on whether the noun they are describing is masculine,
feminine or plural)

e.g. hay <u>muchísimos</u> hoteles en España. - there are <u>lots and lots</u> of hotels in Spain.
e.g. las playas en España son <u>bellísimas</u>. - the beaches in Spain are <u>really lovely</u>.

Note that you need to remove the –´o´ or –´a´ from the adjective before adding the above endings.

Mini Test

1. Book yourself into a luxury room with at least 5 facilities.
2. Imagine yourself in the worst hotel room ever and report all its faults to reception.

Foundation

¿Dónde están los dormitorios?
(Where are the dormitories?)
El dormitorio de chicos está a la izquierda y el dormitorio de chicas está a la derecha.
(The boys' dormitory is on the left and the girls' dormitory is on the right.)

Al camping/At the campsite
¿Hay sitio para una tienda y una caravana?
(Have you got room for a tent and a caravan?)
Sí. ¿Para cuántas noches?
(Yes, for how many nights?)
Para una noche.
(For one night.)

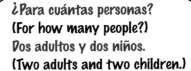

En el Albergue Juvenil/At the Youth Hostel
¿Tiene camas libres para una chica y un chico?
(Have you got room for one girl and one boy?)
Sí. ¿Tienen tarjetas de afiliación?
(Yes, do you have your membership cards?)
Sí.
(Yes)
Vale, hay que rellenar estas fichas.
(OK, you need to fill in these forms.)

¿Para cuántas personas?
(For how many people?)
Dos adultos y dos niños.
(Two adults and two children.)

¿Cuál es la matrícula de su vehículo?
(What is the registration number of your car?)
La matrícula es GBG 390.
(The registration number is GBG 390.)

Es la parcela número 28, al lado de las duchas.
(It's pitch number 28, next to the showers.)

¿Qué hay en este camping?
(What is there on this campsite?)
Hay toma de corriente para caravanas.
(There are electricity points for caravans.)

Vocabulary

el camping	campsite	los aseos	toilets
el albergue juvenil	youth hostel	los cubos de basura	rubbish bins
una tienda	a tent	el salón social	meeting room
una caravana	a caravan	el alojamiento	accommodation
un dormitorio	a dormitory	abierto todo el año	open all year round
un sitio	a place	el aparcamiento	carpark
una parcela	a pitch	un saco de dormir	sleeping bag
sol	sun	la comida	food
sombra	shade	las comidas	meals
la lavandería	laundry	las cerillas	matches
las duchas	showers	el gas butano	camping gas
agua caliente	hot water	un paquete de almuerzo	packed lunch
una toma de corriente	powerpoint	se prohibe	it is forbidden to
un enchufe	plug	agua potable	drinking water

Higher

¿Cuáles son las reglas del albergue juvenil?
(What are the rules of the youth hostel?)
Pues hay que hablar bajo en los dormitorios después de las diez, y cerramos la puerta con llave a medianoche. También si se marcha antes de las ocho hay que pagar la noche anterior.
(Well, you have to speak quietly in the dormitories after ten o' clock and we lock the door at midnight. Also if you leave before eight o' clock you have to pay the night before.)

Me parece que hay un error aquí, dos adultos a cuatrocientas son ochocientas y aquí pone novecientas.
(I think there is a mistake here, two adults at 400 pesetas is 800 pesetas and here it says 900 pesetas.)
Lo siento, tiene razón, lo cambiaré enseguida.
(I'm sorry, you're right, I'll change it straight away.)
Había también algunos problemas, faltaba agua caliente en las duchas y había mucho ruido por la noche.
(There were some problems too, there was no hot water in the showers and there was a lot of noise at night.)

Grammar

Adverbs

Adverbs usually describe verbs but can also be added to adjectives or other adverbs to give you more information. They often end in '-ly' in English. They may stand alone.
Adverbs do not need to agree.

E.g.   Visito España regularmente - I visit Spain regularly.

Formation of Adverbs
To form an adverb from an adjective you need to take the feminine form and add '-mente'.
E.g.   lenta (slow) + mente = lentamente (slowly)

If the adjective does not have a feminine form you just add '-mente' to the masculine form:
E.g.   posible (possible) + mente = posiblemente (possibly)

If you have two adverbs, both ending in '-mente', together you often miss '-mente' off the first one:
E.g.   Conduce lenta y cuidadosamente. - He drives slowly and carefully.

Some are irregular, see list below:

mucho – a lot	muchas veces – often	allí – there
poco – a few/a little	algunas veces – sometimes	aquí – here
bien – well	nunca – never	lejos – far
mal – badly	de vez en cuando – from time to time	enfrente – opposite
rara vez – rarely	cerca – nearby	

Note that 'bastante' and 'demasiado' can be adverbs or adjectives.

Foundation

En la farmacia/At the chemist's

No me siento bien. Estoy muy constipado/a. ¿Puede darme algo?
(I don't feel very well. I've got a bad cold. Can you give me something?)

Sí, la aspirina y estas pastillas son muy buenas.
(Yes, aspirin and these pastilles are very good.)

Si no se siente mejor en dos días debe ir al médico.
(If you don't feel better in two days you need to go to the doctor's.)

¿Tiene algo para una insolación?
(Do you have anything for sunburn?)

Sí, tenemos esta crema para las quemaduras de sol.
(Yes, we have this cream for sunburn.)

¿Cuánto cuesta?
(How much does it cost?)

Cuesta quienientas pesetas.
(It costs 500 pesetas.)

¿Puede darme un recibo?
(Can you give me a receipt?)

Quiero algo para la tos, por favor.
(I'd like something for a cough, please.)

Tome este jarabe tres veces al día.
(Take this cough syrup three times a day.)

Vocabulary

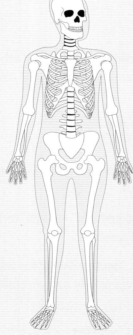

el cuerpo – **the body**	el hombro – **shoulder**
la cabeza – **head**	la espalda – **back**
el cuello – **neck**	el labio – **lip**
el pecho – **chest**	la lengua – **tongue**
el codo – **elbow**	el diente/la muela – **tooth**
el estómago – **stomach**	la muñeca – **wrist**
el muslo – **thigh**	la cintura – **waist**
la pierna – **leg**	
el tobillo – **ankle**	
los dedos del pie – **toes**	la farmacia – **chemist's**
el pie – **foot**	el/la farmacéutico/a – **chemist, pharmacist**
la rodilla – **knee**	un catarro – **a cold**
el pulgar – **thumb**	una tos – **a cough**
los dedos – **fingers**	una fiebre – **a temperature**
la mano – **hand**	una insolación – **sunburn**
el brazo – **arm**	una quemadura – **a burn**
la garganta – **throat**	una picadura – **a bite/sting**
la cara – **face**	un dolor de cabeza – **a headache**
la frente – **forehead**	un dolor – **a pain**
los ojos – **eyes**	cortarse el dedo – **to cut your finger**
la nariz – **nose**	un jarabe – **cough mixture**
la boca – **mouth**	una tirita – **plaster**
las orejas/los oídos – **ears**	una crema – **cream**
la ceja – **eyebrow**	una aspirina – **aspirin**
el mentón – **chin**	una venda – **bandage**
la mejilla – **cheek**	un comprimido – **tablet**

Higher

<u>En la farmacia</u>/**At the chemist's**

Me he cortado el dedo y me duele mucho. ¿Qué me aconseja?

(**I've cut my finger and it really hurts. What do you advise?**)

Puedo darle unas tiritas pero si no mejora debe ir al hospital.

(**I can give you some plasters but if it doesn't improve you should go to the hospital.**)

Me he torcido el tobillo y no puedo andar. ¿Es necesario ver a* un médico?

(**I've sprained my ankle and I can't walk. Do I need to see a doctor?**)

Creo que sería una buena idea.

(**I think it would be a good idea.**)

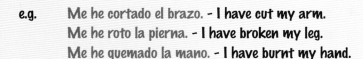

Me ha picado una avispa. ¿Me puede recomendar algo?

(**I've been stung by a wasp. Can you recommend something?**)

Esta crema es muy buena.

(**This cream is very good.**)

*see grammar below

Grammar

Reflexive Verbs with Parts of the Body.

<u>Remember</u> that a REFLEXIVE VERB indicates something that you do to or for yourself. When discussing illnesses and ailments, it is most likely you will be using a reflexive verb with a part of the body in the PERFECT TENSE.

e.g.   Me he cortado el brazo. - **I have cut my arm.**

       Me he roto la pierna. - **I have broken my leg.**

       Me he quemado la mano. - **I have burnt my hand.**

<u>Romperse el brazo</u> – **to break one's arm!**

       Me he roto el brazo – **I have broken my arm.**

       Te has roto el brazo – **You have broken your arm.**

       Se ha roto el brazo – **He/she has broken his/her arm.**

Notice that with parts of the body in Spanish you do not use 'mi' (my) but the definite article 'el/la' (the)

Personal 'a'

This is used in Spanish to distinguish people from objects when you are talking about an action that is happening to them (e.g. phoning them or seeing them). It does not translate into English.

e.g.   Tiene que ver <u>a</u> un médico – **You have to see a doctor.**

       Tiene que llamar <u>a</u> un médico – **You have to call a doctor.**

Foundation

Por teléfono/On the telephone
¿Puede usted darme hora con el médico?
(Can you give me an appointment with the doctor?)
Sí. ¿Puede venir mañana a las diez? ¿Su nombre, por favor?
(Yes, can you come tomorrow at 10 o' clock? Your name please?)

En la clínica del dentista/
At the dentist's
Me duelen las muelas. Perdí un empaste hace tres días.
(I've got toothache. I lost a filling three days ago.)
Voy a ponerle una inyección y después le haré otro empaste.
(I'll give you an injection and then I'll give you another filling.)

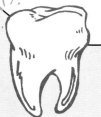

En la clínica/At the clinic
Me duele el estómago y tengo fiebre desde hace dos días.
(I've had stomach ache and a temperature for two days.)
No es nada serio. Voy a recetarle una medicina. Tome una pastilla tres veces al día antes de comer.
(It's nothing serious. I'll give you a prescription. Take one tablet three times a day before meals.)

En la clínica/At the clinic (2)
¿Qué le pasa?
(What is the matter?)
Me duele la espalda.
(My back hurts.)
Vamos a ver. ¿Eso le duele?
(Let's see. Does that hurt?)
Sí, me duele.
(Yes, it hurts.)
Necesita reposo.
(You need to rest it.)

Vocabulary

me duele la cabeza	– I've got a headache	una hora	– appointment
tengo dolor de cabeza	– I've got a headache	una cita	– appointment
me duele la garganta	– I've got a sore throat	una receta	– prescription
estoy mareado/a	– I feel sick/dizzy	un empaste	– filling
me duelen las muelas	– I've got toothache	empastar	– to fill
tengo fiebre	– I've got a temperature	una inyección	– injection
tener calor	– to be hot	hacer un reconocimiento	
tener frío	– to be cold	médico de	– to examine
tener hambre	– to be hungry	tratar	– to treat
tener sed	– to be thirsty	romperse la pierna	– to break one's leg
vomitar	– to vomit	torcerse el tobillo	– to sprain one's ankle
hacerse daño	– to hurt oneself	quemarse la mano	– to burn one's hand
descansar	– to rest	desgarrarse un músculo	– to tear a muscle
guardar cama	– to stay in bed	asmático/a	– asthmatic
serio/a	– serious	una alergia	– allergy
el dolor	– pain	alérgico/a (a)	– allergic (to)
doloroso	– painful		

Higher

En la clínica (1)/At the doctor's (1)

Me he desgarrado un músculo jugando al fútbol.

(I've torn a muscle playing football.)

A ver, tiene hinchada la rodilla.

(Let's see, your knee is swollen.)

Lo sé, no podía dormir por el dolor.

(I know, I couldn't sleep for the pain.)

Le voy a poner una venda y no la mueva.

(I'm going to put a bandage on and you mustn't move it.)

En la clínica (2)/At the doctor's (2)

Me he quemado la mano haciendo la comida.

(I've burnt my hand whilst cooking.)

A ver. ¿Qué pasó exactamente?

(Lets see. What happened exactly?)

Estaba echando agua caliente en una cacerola.

(I was pouring hot water into a saucepan.)

Debe ir al hospital enseguida.

(You must go to hospital straight away.)

Grammar

The Present Participle in Continuous Tenses

The present participle (the verb ending in –ing in English e.g. playing) is formed in the following way in Spanish:

For –AR verbs remove the –AR and add –ANDO

E.g.   Jugar (to play) = jugando (playing)

For –ER and –IR verbs remove the –ER or –IR and add –IENDO

E.g.   Comer (to eat)= comiendo (eating)

Vivir (to live) = viviendo (living)

Remember that the stem will change too for some radical changing verbs:

E.g.   Hervir (to boil) = hir̲viendo (boiling).

There are also some irregular present participles such as;

decir (diciendo - saying), ir (yendo - going), poder (pudiendo – being able to)

The present participle is used with 'estar' in Continuous Tenses,

i.e. where something is or was happening at a particular moment and the action is or was temporary:

Eg.   Está jugando al fútbol. – He is playing football

Estaba jugando al fútbol. – He was playing football.

Mini Test

1. List as many parts of the body as you can in Spanish in one minute.
2. Imagine a conversation with a chemist in Spanish, in which you describe 3 ailments.
   What remedies can be offered?

Foundation

¿Eres deportista?
(Are you sporty?)
Sí, hago ejercicio tres veces a la semana.
(Yes, I exercise three times a week.)

¿Qué hay que beber y comer para estar en forma?
(What should you drink and eat to keep fit?)
Tienes que comer mucha fruta muchas legumbres y beber mucha agua.
(You should eat lots of fruit and vegetables and drink lots of water.)

¿Qué tienes que evitar?
(What should you avoid?)
Tienes que evitar beber demasiado café y no tienes que comer demasiados caramelos.
(You shoud avoid drinking too much coffee and you shouldn't eat too many sweets.)

¿Qué piensas de las drogas?
(What do you think of drugs?)
Son peligrosas, traen muchos riesgos para la salud.
(They are dangerous, there are many risks to one's health.)

¿A qué hora te acuestas?
(At what time do you go to bed?)
Me acuesto temprano durante la semana.
(I go to bed early during the week.)

¿Bebes alcohol?
(Do you drink alcohol?)
De vez en cuando bebo una cerveza.
(From time to time I have a beer.)

¿Fumas?
(Do you smoke?)
No, nunca, es malo para la salud.
(No, never, it's bad for your health.)

Vocabulary

la salud	– health	mantenerse en forma	– to keep fit
sano/a	– healthy	evitar	– to avoid
malsano/a	– unhealthy	las golosinas	– sweet things
hacer ejercicio	– to exercise	la grasa	– fat
el tabaco	– tobacco	la carne	– meat
el alcohol	– alcohol	vegetariano/a	– vegetarian
las drogas	– drugs	relajarse	– to relax
peligroso/a	– dangerous	el estrés	– stress
asqueroso/a	– disgusting	los granos	– spots
de vez en cuando	– from time to time	la depresión	– depression
con moderación	– in moderation	deprimido/a	– depressed
regularmente	– regularly	el cansancio	– tiredness
rara vez	– rarely	el apetito	– appetite
temprano/a	– early	el riesgo	– risk
tarde	– late	la enfermedad	– illness
estar en forma	– to be fit/healthy	la adicción	– addiction

Higher

¿Qué haces para mantenerte en forma?
(What do you do to keep fit?)
Hago ejercicio regularmente – natación,
baile y yoga y como sanamente.
(I exercise regularly – swimming, dancing
and yoga and I eat healthily.)

¿Cuáles son los riesgos de tomar
drogas?
(What are the risks of taking drugs?)
Hay siempre un riesgo de adicción y para los
que se inyectan hay el riesgo del Sida.
(There is always a risk of addiction and
for those who inject themselves there
is the risk of Aids.)

¿Qué quiere decir 'como sanamente'?
(What does that mean 'I eat healthily'?)
No como mucha carne y trato de evitar las
golosinas y la grasa.
(I don't eat much meat and I try to
avoid sweet things and fat.)

DRUGS ARE NOT COOL!

JUST SAY NO!

¿Por qué fuma la gente o
bebe alcohol en tu opinión?
(Why do people smoke or
drink alcohol in your
opinion?)
Por curiosidad o porque les
hace sentirse mayor.
(Out of curiosity or because
it makes them feel more
grown up.)

¿Qué haces para relajarte?
(What do you do to relax?)
Para relajarme y evitar el estrés
escucho música o llamo a una amiga.
(To relax and avoid stress, I listen
to music or I call a friend.)

Grammar

Giving Advice

This is an appropriate topic in which to look at GIVING ADVICE in Spanish.
The following expressions are all used with an infinitive and all express the idea of
'having to' or 'must':

Tener que – this is the most forceful of the three
Hay que – is the next most forceful
Deber (de) – is the weakest of the three. It is followed by 'de' when you are making an assumption.

E.g. Tienes que beber mucha agua. – You must drink lots of water.
Hay que comer mucha fruta. – You ought to eat lots of fruit.
No debes fumar. – You shouldn't smoke.
Debe de estar en forma. – He must be fit (assumption).

Mini Test

Make a list of healthy and unhealthy things about your lifestyle. Make 5 resolutions to improve it.

Foundation

¿Que problemas hay en tu barrio?
(What problems are there in your area?)
Hay mucho tráfico en las carreteras, y eso contamina el medio ambiente.
(There is a lot of traffic on the roads and this pollutes the environment.)

¿Qué piensas del reciclaje?
(What do you think of recycling?)
Pienso que es una buena idea para conservar los recursos naturales.
(I think that it is a good idea to conserve natural resources.)

¿Cómo se puede mejorar la ciudad/el pueblo?
(How can the town/village be improved?)
Hacen falta más autobuses y hay que reducir el tráfico.
(We need more buses and they should limit the traffic.)

¿Qué más te molesta?
(What else bothers you?)
Me molesta también que no hay suficientes servicios para los minusválidos.
(It also bothers me that there aren't enough facilities for the handicapped.)

¿Hay otros problemas que te preocupen?
(Are there any other problems which worry you?)
Sí, el barrio está muy sucio y siempre hay papeles en el suelo.
(Yes, the area is very dirty and there is always litter on the ground.)

¿Cuál es el problema más importante para tí?
(What is the most important problem for you?)
Me preocupo por los sin techo.
(I worry about the homeless.)

Vocabulary

el medio ambiente	– the environment	la sequía	– drought
el tráfico	– traffic	la caza	– hunting
la circulación	– traffic	la sobrepesca	– overfishing
la contaminación	– pollution	economizar	– to economise
los desperdicios	– rubbish	proteger	– to protect
las ventajas	– advantages	cuidar	– to look after
las desventajas	– disadvantages	mejorar	– to improve
el reciclaje	– recycling	malgastar	– to waste
reciclar	– to recycle	estropear	– to spoil
la deforestación	– deforestation	molestar	– to bother
la superpoblación	– overpopulation	preocuparse por	– to worry about
la capa de ozono	– the ozone layer	inquietarse	– to worry
la destrucción	– destruction	fastidiar	– to annoy

Higher

¿Cuáles son los problemas más graves para nuestra sociedad hoy?
(What are the most serious problems for our society today?)
En mi opinión el gobierno debe asumir responsibilidad por los parados.
(In my opinion the government should take responsibility for the unemployed.)

¿Qué piensas de algunos problemas como, por ejemplo, el agujero en la capa de ozono y el efecto invernadero?
(What do you think of problems such as, for example, the hole in the ozone layer and the greenhouse effect?)
Pienso que cada persona debe hacer algo para ayudar si queremos mejorar la situación.
(I think that everyone should do something to help if we want to improve the situation.)

¿Qué opinas de los problemas del tercer mundo. Es nuestra responsibilidad ayudar a esta gente también?
(What do you think of the problems in the third world. Is it our responsibility to help these people too?)
Creo que seríamos egoístas si dijéramos que no tiene nada que ver con nosotros sólo porque no vivimos allí. Siempre debemos ayudar cuando se trata de un problema.
(I think we would be selfish if we said that it had nothing to do with us just because we don't live there. We should always help when there is a problem.)

Grammar

Verbs followed by an Infinitive
In Spanish some verbs are followed by a straight infinitive, others require a preposition such as 'a' or 'de' before the infinitive.

E.g.   Quiero estar en forma. – **I want to be fit.**   Trato de evitar la grasa. – **I try to avoid fat.**
       Empiezo a hacer más ejercicio. – **I am starting to exercise more.**

You need to learn which verbs are followed by 'a', 'de' or just an infinitive.

Here are a few useful ones:

+ infinitive
gustar – **to like to**	poder – **to be able to**	querer – **to want to**	deber – **to have to**
decidir – **to decide to**	intentar – **to try to**	necesitar – **to need to**	esperar – **to hope to**
preferir – **to prefer to**	saber – **to know how to**		

+ de + infinitive
Tratar de – **to try to**	acordarse de – **to remember to**	olvidarse de – **to forget to**
acabar de – **to have just...**	terminar de – **to finish ...-ing**	

+ a + infinitive
aprender a – **to learn to**	ayudar a – **to help to**	empezar a – **to begin to**
invitar a – **to invite to**	forzar a – **to force to**	ponerse a – **to set about...-ing**

You will find the following phrases useful when conversing in Spanish:

Perdón	–	Sorry
Lo siento	–	I'm sorry
No entiendo (muy bien)	–	I don't understand (very well)
¿Puede hablar más despacio?	–	Can you speak more slowly?
¿Puede repetirlo?	–	Can you repeat it?
Deletrear	–	To spell
Explicar	–	To explain
¿Cómo se escribe?	–	How do you spell it?
¿Puede deletrearlo?	–	Can you spell it?
Hablo español un poco/bastante bien/bien/muy bien	–	I speak Spanish a bit/quite well/well/very well
No lo sé	–	I don't know
¿Me entiendes/me entiende?	–	Do you understand me?
¿Qué quiere decir...?	–	What does... mean?
¿Cómo se dice... en español?	–	How do you say... in Spanish?
¿Cómo se dice... en inglés?	–	How do you say... in English?
Perdóneme	–	Excuse me
Con permiso	–	Excuse me (when passing someone)
¡Hola!	–	Hello!
Buenos días	–	Good day
Buenas tardes	–	Good afternoon/Good evening
Buenas noches	–	Goodnight
Hasta luego	–	See you later
Hasta pronto	–	See you soon
¿Qué tal?	–	How are you?
¿Qué pasa?	–	How are you (informal)
Bien gracias	–	Fine thanks
Muchas gracias	–	Thank you very much
De nada	–	Don't mention it
Por favor	–	Please
Verdad o mentira	–	True or False
No dice	–	It doesn't say
No menciona	–	It doesn't mention
Lee	–	Read
La carta	–	The letter
El artículo	–	The article

The majority of instructions on your Spanish exam papers will be in the target language. The following list is not exhaustive, but will help to illustrate the kind of instructions likely to be encountered.

Mira	–	Look at
Los dibujos	–	The pictures
Las fotos	–	The photos
Escribe (unas...palabras)	–	Write (about... words)
Decide	–	Decide
Elige	–	Choose
Describe	–	Describe
Completa	–	Complete
Contesta	–	Answer
Ordena	–	Put in order
Rellena los espacios	–	Fill in the gaps
Una casilla	–	A box
Indica con una seña	–	Tick
En español	–	In Spanish
En inglés	–	In English
Haz una lista	–	Make a list
Explica	–	Explain
Compara	–	Compare
Por ejemplo	–	For example
Empareja	–	Match up
Una letra	–	A letter
Una cifra	–	A number/figure
¡te toca a ti!	–	Your turn!

Specific to Listening:

Escucha la cinta	–	Listen to the tape
Se repite dos veces	–	It will be repeated twice
Habrá una pausa	–	There will be a pause

Specific to oral:

Pregunta	–	Ask
Habla	–	Speak
Saluda al examinador(a)	–	Greet the examiner
Empieza la conversación	–	Start the conversation
Haz una pregunta	–	Ask a question
Termina la conversación	–	Finish the conversation

Notes

You will normally be required to express yourself in two different ways:

a) In a situation that you might encounter while on holiday in the country – e.g. bank, shop, café.

b) Talking about yourself.

Role Play

1. Está usted en un banco. Es usted el cliente. El profesor es el empleado del banco. (i)

   (You are in a bank. You are the customer. The teacher is the bank employee.)

a.) Ask if you can change some travellers cheques. (ii)

a)

b)

b.) Ask what the exchange rate is.

c.) Ask if you have to pay commission. (iii)

c)

d)

d.) (!) (iv)

e.) Say thank you and goodbye. (v)

e)

Role Play Notes

You are unlikely to know what this situation is until the day of the exam, but if you have revised well and learnt some stock phrases and key vocabulary you should easily be able to cope. You should also make sure that you understand the different question words. You will have some time to prepare .

(i) Make sure that you appreciate where the situation is taking place (the bank), and who is who (you are the customer). Also note the use of 'usted' as this is a formal situation.

(ii) Think what you actually need to say: ('I would like to change some travellers cheques'), remember you are unlikely to be able to look up 'I would like' as it is part of a verb – this is where your memory comes in!

(iii) Even if you cannot manage to say the whole sentence, say what you can – even if it is just one or two words like 'pagar', 'comisión', you will be given credit for knowing the key words.

(iv) Part of the exam may require you to think on your feet and reply spontaneously to the examiner, this is where it is useful if you understand all the question words. It is quite often easy to anticipate what the question will be e.g. here it could be something like, 'do you have any ID?'

(v) Don't give up! Even if you feel you have not done your best on the rest of the conversation, make sure you finish it off. You will always get marks for communication.

Conversation

You will be expected to speak about two of the topics listed below, you may well not find out which topics until the day of the exam, so you will need to be ready to speak about any of them. Depending on whether you are sitting Foundation Level or Higher Level, the topics will be written in English or Spanish on your card.

Self, family, friends and leisure – Tú, tu familia, tus amigos y tu tiempo libre (i)
House, home and region – Tu casa y tu región (ii)
School and daily routine – Tu colegio y tu rutina diaria (iii)

Future plans (e.g. 16+, work, careers) – Tus proyectos para el futuro (iv)
Work (e.g. spending money, temporary work, work experience) – El trabajo
Health (e.g. lifestyle, smoking, alcohol, drugs) – La salud (v)

Conversation Notes

All of these sections have been dealt with in this revision guide. You do not want to waste valuable preparation time – make sure you are well prepared in advance.

(i)   Whatever your topics are, you need to think carefully how you can exploit them to their utmost if you need to speak for between 2-4 minutes (Foundation) or 5-7 minutes (Higher). You should also think about how you can bring in different tenses and more advanced constructions if you are sitting the Higher Level.

(ii)   Your teacher/examiner will prompt you with questions if you dry up, but you should try to give as much detail as possible and take the initiative to move on to talking about another aspect of the topic. Don't worry if you forget something, keep going, the more you say the better.

(iii)   Aim to use a variety of vocabulary, constructions and tenses throughout if you can.
        Also remember to try hard with your pronunciation and accent, even if it seems over the top to you.

(iv)   This is an obvious topic for the use of different tenses, you do not, however, need to limit yourself to the future tense you can also bring in past experiences and link them to your future plans. It is up to you whether you keep it simple and accurate or if you want to be a little bit more adventurous and original.

(v)   This is a particularly good section for expressing your views and opinions on a few general topics, aim for some variey rather than keep repeating 'pienso que...'. Try to keep cool and don't rush your answers, your teacher/examiner will help you if you get stuck.

Remember you do not have to tell the truth - no one will check! Have a look at the relevant sections of the guide for some ideas.

The best preparation for this part of the GCSE assessment is to listen to as much spoken Spanish as you can:

- Radio.
- Satellite television.
- A trip to Spain/School exchange
- Exchanging cassettes with a Spanish penfriend.
- The use of listening materials from school.

Together with this, of course, you must have a sound base of Spanish vocabulary across the topic areas. At Foundation Level you can expect to hear announcements, instructions, requests, dialogues, short news items. In fact, there is a good deal of overlap between the vocabulary and phrases needed for the oral role-play situations and Foundation Level listening material. At Higher Level you can expect to hear longer and more complex passages. Some points to bear in mind for your listening exam:

- Before the exam, familiarise yourself with instructions in Spanish (see page 71).
- Look carefully at any examples given.
- Always read the questions in advance so that you know what type of information you are listening for.

e.g. <u>question:</u>   ¿A qué hora se levanta el sábado?

<u>You hear:</u> Normalmente durante la semana me levanto a las seis y media. Me ducho, me visto y desayuno en la cocina, salgo de casa a las siete y media. <u>El sábado</u>, me levanto más tarde – <u>a las nueve</u>.

Only the information underlined is required to answer the question. The rest can be ignored.

Remember that you will hear the item more than once, and that you can make notes throughout.

- Do not worry, particularly at Higher Level, if you do not understand every single word. Again, concentrate on listening out for the information required by the question.

- Check how many marks a question is worth, if the whole question is worth 11 marks you know that you need to tick 11 boxes or provide 11 pieces of information.

- Check if answers have to be written in Spanish or English. Remember that you do not have to answer in full sentences, and that Spanish answers will not be marked for accuracy, only comprehension.

- If asked to tick 3 boxes, do not tick more than 3, in the hope that you may have the 3 correct answers amongst all your ticks! You will be penalised if you do this.

- Similarly, do not leave a question unanswered. There are no marks awarded for a blank space, but an intelligent guess may gain you marks.

The reading assessment is based on a range of written texts, varying in length and complexity, for example, from a short public notice to a magazine or newspaper article. Much of the advice for the listening exam is also relevant here.

- Read the titles and questions carefully. They often provide a helpful context.

- Scan the text for information related to the question, and then go back to the question – what exactly is required?

- Sometimes, especially with longer items, the trick is to understand the gist, the general idea, and not every single word.

- Sometimes it is a matter of finding the relevant bit of information in a longer passage, where you are not expected or required to understand everything.

- Sometimes the answer hinges on one little word, which you must be careful not to overlook,
  e.g. 'el museo está abierto todos los días <u>salvo</u> el martes'

Some candidates will read 'todos los días' (every day) and think they have found the answer regarding the museum's hours and days of opening, missing the vital word 'salvo' (except). Make sure your revision includes a list of these short but very important words!

- Sometimes you will be expected to deduce meaning from the context, which may provide a clue:
  'el béisbol, un deporte americano'
  'un deporte' should help you to realise that 'el béisbol' is a type of sport. From there you should be able to see the similarity between 'béisbol' and 'baseball'.

- Use clues offered by the language and grammar of the text; you will need to be able to recognise different tenses, singular and plural nouns and verbs, feminine and plural agreements, etc.
  e.g. the following words are provided for this gap-filling exercise:

  deportistas / ir / voy / él / árbol / casa

  a.) los hermanos de Sonia son más .... que ella. (adjective with masculine plural agreement required)
  b.) Es una .... española. (feminine noun required)
  c.) Quiero .... al extranjero. (infinitive required)

- Be aware of words which look similar to an English word but have a different meaning in Spanish e.g. 'sensible' does not mean 'sensible' as you might assume but 'sensitive'.

- Please read the section on the use of a Spanish/English dictionary, in order to help you to avoid the pitfalls (see page 81)

<u>For specific details of the listening and reading assessments you will need to check the requirements of your own syllabus.</u>

Foundation

You may be required to fill out a form or leave someone a note at Foundation Level:

A FORM

e.g. - Has perdido algo. Tienes que rellenar este formulario (i)

		marks
Fecha (ii)	El doce de agosto	(1)
Apellido/nombre (iii)	Taylor Ken	(2)
Artículo perdido	Una cartera	(1)
Descripción (iv)	De piel, negra, contiene cinco mil pesetas	(3)
Sitio exacto (v)	En el aeropuerto	(2)
Domicilio	Hotel Miramar, Calle de la Playa Benidorm	(1)

Notes On Filling Out Forms

(i)   As always, make sure you understand the instructions (filling out a lost property form). Notice that they have left it up to you to decide what you have lost.

(ii)   Try to include some Spanish if you can rather than just putting the date in numbers.

(iii)   Make sure you get your names the right way round.

(iv)   This is your opportunity to include as much detail as possible. Check how many marks are available so that you can be sure to include enough information. Notice that it can be in note form rather than full sentences.

(v)   Remember to add the word for 'at' or 'in'.

A NOTE

e.g. - La familia no está en casa y tu tienes que salir. Escribe un mensaje para la familia (i). Escribe unas 25 palabras (ii).

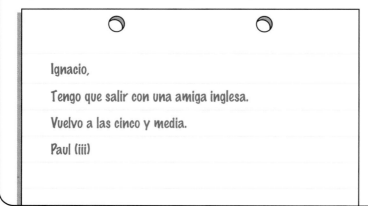

Ignacio,

Tengo que salir con una amiga inglesa.

Vuelvo a las cinco y media.

Paul (iii)

Notes On Writing Notes!

You may be required to write a note to a friend.

(i) Once you have decided what you need to do, have a look at the instructions to see if there are any phrases you can use. You may need to change them around a bit.

e.g. <u>tienes</u> que salir - you have to go out
<u>tengo</u> que salir - I have to go out

(ii) Notice how many words you need to write. This is never an exact amount but you may be penalised if your work is too short or too long; try to stay within 5 words either way on shorter tasks.

(iii) You should always check your work. A check list should include: spellings, genders, accents, agreements, verb endings, tenses.

Higher

A LETTER TO A FRIEND

e.g. - Escribe una carta a tu amigo/a español(a). Describe las vacaciones que acabas de pasar con tu familia (i). Escribe unas 100 palabras.

Sutton Coldfield, catorce de agosto de 2000 (ii)

Querida Raquel, (iii)

Te escribo para contarte (iv) mis vacaciones en Nueva York con mi familia. Salimos (v) a las tres de la madrugada del aeropuerto de Birmingham. ¡Qué pronto! (vi) ¡Levantarme antes de las nueve! Además (vii), como sabes, tengo miedo a los aviones pero escuché música y dormí un poco y no fue tan malo. Nos quedamos en un gran (viii) hotel de cinco estrellas, lo encontré muy impresionante (ix). Comí hamburguesas todos los días porque son más sabrosas allí en Estados Unidos que en Inglaterra (x). ¿Y tú? ¿Adónde fuiste de vacaciones? (xi)

Un abrazo, tu amiga (xii)
Rebecca

Notes On Writing Informal Letters

(i)   Make sure you work out which tense you are being required to use (past here to describe holidays you've just been on), and whether the letter is formal (use 'usted') or informal (use 'tú').

(ii)   Remember that in Spanish you only need to head your letter with the place from which you are writing and the date.

(iii)   Make sure you have an appropriate beginning (querido/querida depending on who you are writing to).

(iv)   You need an opening sentence to introduce the letter. Using an indirect object pronoun ('te') is impressive.

(v)   Check your past tense, have you got the correct one? (preterite here).

(vi)   Using idiomatic expressions such as, '¡qué pronto!' (How early!) shows that you have a good knowledge of the language.

(vii)   Little linking words such as 'además' (what's more) help to increase the variety of the vocabulary you use and to make your sentences more complex.

(viii)   Use adjectives whenever you can, remember to check for agreements.

(ix)   Give opinions wherever possible.

(x)   Using comparatives will also help to improve your marks for quality of language.

(xi)   Add a question, again it is a technique which will impress examiners – don't forget the inverted punctuation at the beginning of a question or exclamation in Spanish.

(xii)   Make sure that you finish with an appropriate ending such as 'un abrazo' (best wishes). Check that your letter is the correct length. Check your work thoroughly (see note (iii) page 77).

Higher

A FORMAL LETTER

e.g. - Escriba una carta al hotel donde se quedó de vacaciones para quejarse del estado de la habitación (i).

Escriba unas 100 palabras.

> 25 Gloucester Road (ii)
>
> Cannock
>
> Staffordshire
>
> WS11 3SR
>
> veinticinco de julio de 2000
>
> Muy señor mío, (iii)
>
> Acabo de regresar (iv) de vacaciones en Alicante donde pasamos dos semanas inolvidables. Desafortunadamente, (v) nos quedamos muy insatisfechos del estado de la habitación en su hotel. No había (vi) toallas en el cuarto de baño y no cambiaron las sábanas durante las dos semanas. La ventana estaba rota (vii) y no funcionaba la ducha. Hacían falta perchas para la ropa y cuando hablamos con la recepcionista nos (viii) dijo que no había más.
>
> En espera de su pronta respuesta
>
> Le saluda atentamente (ix)
>
> J. Singh

Notes On Writing Formal Letters

(i)   Notice that you are required to write a formal letter of complaint (use 'usted') in the past tense; notice the use of the imperfect tense for description (of the room) in the past.

(ii)   You will need to give your full address as you expect a reply.

(iii)   Use an appropriate beginning for a business letter 'muy señor mío' (Dear Sir).

(iv)   Again note the use of idiomatic expressions where the Spanish uses a different tense with 'acabar de' (to have just...).

(v)   Using adverbs will help your marks for language used.

(vi)   Use the imperfect tense to describe the state of the room.

(vii)   Using past participles as adjectives shows a good understanding of the language.

(viii)   Again the use of indirect object pronouns (nos) shows how well you can manipulate the language.

(ix)   It is worth learning a set expression such as this for 'yours faithfully'.

Higher

AN ARTICLE/ESSAY

e.g. – Decides ayudar a tu amigo español con sus deberes, tiene que escribir un artículo sobre las ventajas y las desventajas de vivir en una ciudad **(i)**. Escribe unas 120 palabras.

MI CIUDAD

Vivo en una gran ciudad inglesa que **(ii)** se llama Leeds. Leeds está **(iii)** en el norte de Inglaterra y es una ciudad industrial. Vivo en Leeds desde mi nacimiento y es una ciudad que me encanta.

Por una parte **(iv)** hay muchas ventajas, sobre todo por la noche. Siempre hay algo interesante que hacer y es una ciudad muy animada. Si te gusta salir de copas o a un restaurante o a ver una película, tienes un gran surtido.

Por otra parte **(iv)**, hay también desventajas. Por ejemplo **(iv)**, hay demasiado tráfico y por lo tanto hay mucha contaminación. Los parques están sucios y por la noche es peligroso andar por algunos barrios.

Sin embargo, a pesar de las desventajas, prefiero vivir en la ciudad, quizás porque estoy acostumbrada pero también a causa de las oportunidades que existen aquí **(v)**.

Notes On Articles And Essays

(i)   You need to think about your layout and structure for an article such as this. Don't forget to give it a title – in Spanish! If you have a title which asks you for the pros and cons of something you should try to give a balanced account. Normally you will need 4 short paragraphs (120 words isn't that much): an introduction, a paragraph for, a paragraph against and a conclusion where you decide which point of view you agree with.

(ii)   Think about using relative pronouns to link your sentences enabling you to make them more complex.

(iii)   Be careful with the use of 'ser' and 'estar' – estar here as you are talking about geographical location.

(iv)   These sort of linking words are common in an article of this type and are useful for bringing in counter arguments or to illustrate a point.

(v)   Make sure that you back up your conclusion with a reason why; you should be able to justify your opinions.

The use of a Spanish/English dictionary for GCSE can be a mixed blessing. It can help with reading comprehension, and in the production of written Spanish. You must, however, take care to learn words that you have looked up as you will not be allowed to use a dictionary during the exam.

You need to bear the following in mind when using your dictionary.

Avoid the temptation to look up every single word. When alternative Spanish words are offered in your dictionary, check each one in the Spanish to English section to find the one with the correct meaning:

e.g. English 'lead' – do you want... ...plomo m.?

...delantera f.?

...pista f.?

...cuerda f.?

...llevar?

...dirigir?

...ir primero?

Be aware that the different structures of Spanish and English do not allow for word to word translation. You need a sound understanding of the rules of grammar and sentence structure.

Be aware of words which are similar to English, Spanish often just adds an -o.

e.g.   aspecto - aspect

        automático - automatic

Some words just add an -e.

e.g.   aire - air

Some English words ending in -y end in -ía or -ia in Spanish.

e.g.   biología - biology

Remember that ph- in English will often be f- in Spanish.

e.g.   filosofía - philosophy

Where English uses th- Spanish often uses just t-.

e.g.   theatre - teatro

Spanish adverbs ending in -mente correspond to English adverbs ending in -ly.

e.g.   generalmente - generally

Words ending in -tion in English end in -ción in Spanish.

e.g.   acción - action

Des- in Spanish is often replaced by dis- in English.

e.g.   desconectar - disconnect

Spanish words ending in -dad correspond to English words ending in -ty.

e.g.   sociedad - society

NOUNS

Nouns in Spanish are either masculine (el) or feminine (la). When you look a word up in a dictionary 'n.m.' means 'noun – masculine' and 'n.f.' means 'noun – feminine'
e.g.
man - hombre (n.m.)

woman - mujer (n.f.)

PLURAL NOUNS

Plural nouns are usually formed by adding an 's' to the singular if it ends in a vowel, or 'es' if it ends in a consonant.
e.g.
un hombre - los hombre<u>s</u>

una mujer - las muj<u>er</u>es

Some words lose or add an accent in the plural eg. el jardín <u>but</u> los jardines.
Some words change their spelling from 'z' to 'c' and then add 'es' eg. el lapiz <u>but</u> los lápices.

ACCENTS

The stress generally falls on the last but one syllable in a Spanish word of more than one syllable which ends in a vowel, 'n' or 's' e.g. casa. Otherwise the last syllable is stressed e.g. ciudad. An accent will indicate any variation from this rule, e.g. lápiz.

DEFINITE ARTICLE

The definite article el, la, los, las is equivalent to the English 'the' and is used when you are referring to something specific or definite.
e.g.
el gato - the cat

la casa - the house

los perros - the dogs

las patatas - the potatoes

You will always need to use an article before a noun in Spanish except when:

- you don't specify an amount – hay tiendas en mi pueblo - there are shops in my village
- you use a negative – no tengo hermanos - I don't have any brothers
- you are saying what someone's job is – soy profesor - I am a teacher

*note that for feminine nouns beginning with a stressed –a or –ha, la is replaced by el e.g. el aula (n.f.), however, it will still need a feminine adjective.

INDEFINITE ARTICLE

The indefinite article un, una, unos, unas is equivalent to the English 'a', 'an' or 'some':
e.g.
un coche - a car

una vaca - a cow

unos libros - some books

unas tiendas - some shops

'A' OR 'DE' WITH DEFINITE ARTICLE

Note that 'a' and 'de' + the masculine singular definite article (el) combine as follows:

A + el = al
De + el = del

ADJECTIVES

Adjectives and agreements, see page 11
Adjectives ending in –ísimo, lo + adjective see p58

If you want to combine two adjectives in a sentence use 'y'
e.g. tiene el pelo largo y rizado - she has long curly hair

POSSESSIVE ADJECTIVES

These show possession and agree with the noun that they describe.

Masculine singular	Feminine singular	Masculine plural	Feminine plural	
mi	mi	mis	mis	= my
tu	tu	tus	tus	= your
su	su	sus	sus	= his,her, its,your(formal)
nuestro	nuestra	nuestros	nuestras	= our
vuestro	vuestra	vuestros	vuestras	= your (plural)
su	su	sus	sus	= their/your(formal)

e.g. es mi mochila - it's my rucksack
son nuestros cuadernos - they are our exercise books

These are not usually used with parts of the body or clothes.

COMPARATIVE AND SUPERLATIVE OF ADJECTIVES

See page 25

Note that when you use más or menos with a number to mean 'more than' you need to use 'de' instead of 'que'
e.g. hay más de dos mil habitantes en mi pueblo - there are more than 2,000 inhabitants in my village

'menor' and 'mayor' meaning younger and older can also be used to mean smaller and bigger

With superlatives, if the adjective follows the noun immediately you leave out the 'el', 'la', 'los', 'las'
e.g. la montaña más alta del mundo - the highest mountain in the world

DEMONSTRATIVE ADJECTIVE

Este, ese, aquel, see page 46

ADVERBS

See page 61 for formation of adverbs.
Note that 'bastante' and 'demasiado' can act as an adjective or an adverb:
e.g. hay demasiada gente - there are too many people
Demasiado needs to agree when used as an adjective
e.g. he comido demasiado - I have eaten too much
It doesn't need to agree when used as an adverb

COMPARATIVE OF ADVERBS

e.g. habla despacio. - He speaks slowly

To make a comparison you need to use 'más' (more) or 'menos' (less) before the adverb and 'que' (than) after it.
e.g. habla más despacio que su hermano - he speaks more slowly than his brother

Note the following irregular comparatives:

bien (well)	mejor (better)
mal (badly)	peor (worse)
mucho (a lot)	más (more)
poco (little)	menos (less)

VERBS - INFINITIVES

Remember that this is the verb as it is found in the dictionary.
There are three categories of endings -AR, -ER and -IR.
This will determine their endings in the present (see pages 13 and 15)
Irregular verbs such as 'ser' (see page 9) must be learnt as they do not conform to these patterns.

For verbs followed by an infinitive see page 69.

You can also make a verb do the work of a noun by giving it a masculine gender:
e.g.   el hablar esta prohibido aquí - speaking is forbidden here

TENSES

Verbs in Spanish have different endings and forms depending on the tense and subject of the verb,
(yo, tú, él etc.). It is extremely important that you get the correct ending for the correct
person as pronouns are not generally used to indicate who you are talking about.
e.g.   vivo - I live

PRESENT TENSE

Examples of regular -AR, -ER and -IR verbs in the present tense are given on pages 13 and 15,
examples of radical changing verbs in the present tense are given on page 21.

PRESENT CONTINUOUS TENSE

This tense is used to indicate what is happening at the time of speaking, or when one action is happening at the same time as another.

It is formed by taking the present tense of 'estar' (see page 31) and the present participle of the main verb (see page 65).

e.g.

estoy jugando al tenis	- I am playing tennis
está hablando con mi madre	- he is talking to my mother
están comiendo patatas fritas	- they are eating chips

IRREGULAR VERBS

A number of common verbs in Spanish are irregular, i.e. they do not follow the normal pattern. The present tense of tener, ser, estar, hacer and ir can be found in the guide on pages 9, 31, and 15 respectively. A good dictionary or grammar reference will provide an irregular verb table.

SER AND ESTAR

These two verbs both mean 'to be' depending on the circumstances.
They feature in the guide on pages 9 and 31.

Here are a few rules to help you to decide which one to use:

Ser is the 'permanent' verb. It is used when you are talking about professions, nationalities, personality, character and is also used for facts that cannot change and for times, dates and numbers.

e.g.

es abogado	- he is a lawyer
son las cinco	- it is 5 o' clock
soy generosa	- I am generous
eres español	- you are Spanish
es cinco de enero	- it is the 5th of January

Estar is the temporary verb. It is used to indicate position or location or when the condition you are talking about is likely to change, for example a change of mood or health or state.

e.g.

Sevilla está en el sur de España	- Seville is in the south of Spain
María está enferma hoy	- María is ill today
De momento está soltero	- at the moment he is single

REFLEXIVE VERBS

- Present tense see page 19
- Perfect tense see page 63

The reflexive pronoun always comes before the verb unless the reflexive verb is in the infinitive in which case it is joined onto the infinitive and needs to change depending on the person that you are referring to.

e.g. <u>me</u> lavo el pelo - I wash my hair

<u>but</u> quiere lavar<u>se</u> el pelo - she wants to wash her hair

SE can also be used with a verb in the third person to form an impersonal construction.

e.g. se vende vino aquí - wine is sold here

se habla español - Spanish is spoken

This can also be used to make general statements or questions and avoids using the passive.

e.g. ¿Dónde se puede comprar recuerdos? - where can one buy souvenirs?

se come mucha paella en España - they eat a lot of paella in Spain

THE IMPERATIVE - COMMANDS

See page 39, for positive commands (formal and informal).

Notice the use of the upside down exclamation mark before a command.

Some irregular verbs have an irregular tú form:

Decir (to say, tell) = di

Hacer (to do, make) = haz

Ir (to go) = ve

Poner (to put) = pon

Salir (to go out) = sal

Ser (to be) = sé

Tener (to have) = ten

Venir (to come) = ven

Negative Commands

Used to tell someone not to do something. These all use the present subjunctive.

<u>Tú</u>

eg.

¡no hables! - don't talk!

¡no bebas el vino! - don't drink the wine!

¡no salgas! - don't go out!

<u>usted</u>

e.g.

¡no hable! - don't talk!

¡no beba el vino! - don't drink the wine!

¡no salga! - don't go out!

THE PRETERITE TENSE

See page 29 for how to form the preterite tense.

It is used to indicate an action which began and ended in the past.

The most common irregular verbs in this tense are:

Dar	–	to give	Di	–	I gave
Estar	–	to be	Estuve	–	I was
Hacer	–	to do, make	Hice	–	I did, made
Ir	–	to go	Fui	–	I went*
Poder	–	to be able to	Pude	–	I was able to
Poner	–	to put	Puse	–	I put
Ser	–	to be	Fui	–	I was*
Tener	–	to have	Tuve	–	I had
Ver	–	to see	Vi	–	I saw
Venir	–	to come	Vine	–	I came

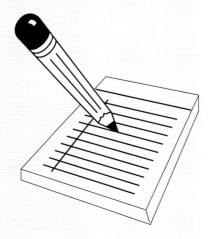

Notice that 'ser' and 'ir' have the same form in this tense, the meaning is usually obvious through context.

e.g. fui al bar – I went to the bar
 fui carpintero – I was a carpenter

Some verbs change their spelling in the first person (I)

c ⟶ que: tocar = toqué
g ⟶ gu: jugar = jugué

Some radical changing verbs change in the he/she/you (usted)/they/you (ustedes) forms:

e ⟶ i: vestir – vistió/vistieron
o ⟶ u: dormir – durmió/durmieron

THE PERFECT TENSE

See page 33 for the formation of this tense.

This tense describes an action which happened within the period of time that the speaker is describing. It is also used for questions that do not refer to any particular time.

Some common irregular past participles:

Abrir (to open)	Abierto	Morir (to die)	Muerto
Cubrir (to cover)	Cubierto	Poner (to put)	Puesto
Decir (to say, tell)	Dicho	Romper (to break)	Roto
Escribir (to write)	Escrito	Ver (to see)	Visto
Hacer (to do, make)	Hecho	Volver (to return)	Vuelto

THE PLUPERFECT TENSE

The pluperfect tense is used to indicate an action that had happened and was completed before another action took place in the past, it is usually denoted by HAD in English.

e.g. había terminado mis deberes cuando llamó mi amigo - I <u>had</u> finished my homework when my friend phoned

The pluperfect is formed in a similar way to the perfect tense, with a past participle and part of 'haber' in the IMPERFECT tense:

> había - I had
> habías - you had
> había - he/she/it/ you (formal) had
> habíamos - we had
> habíais - you had
> habían - they/you (formal) had

THE CONDITIONAL PERFECT

This is used to translate the English 'would have' and its formation is very similar to the pluperfect tense:
You need the CONDITIONAL TENSE of HABER:

Habría, habrías, habría, habríamos, habríais, habrían

+ the past participle: COMPRADO, COMIDO, VIVIDO

e.g.   habría comprado la falda - I would have bought the skirt
   habrían comido toda la paella - they would have eaten all the paella
   habría vivido al extranjero - he would have lived abroad

as its title suggests it usually depends on a condition (if...)

THE IMPERFECT TENSE

See page 43 for its formation and use.

Notice these 3 exceptions:

Ser	Ir	Ver
era	iba	veía
eras	ibas	veías
era	iba	veía
éramos	íbamos	veíamos
erais	ibais	veíais
eran	iban	veían

It is used in three main situations:

a)   to describe an action which used to happen regularly in the past (i.e. to translate the English 'used to'):
   e.g. jugaba en el parque cuando era niño - I used to play in the park when I was a child.

b)   To describe an incomplete action in the past, often used to set the scene:
   e.g. iba al cine cuando ... - I was going to the cinema when ...

c)   To describe certain things in the past, for example: people, places, clothes, hair, weather and feelings.
   e.g. era bonita, tenía el pelo corto y rubio y llevaba un vestido azul.
   - she was pretty, she had short blonde hair and she was wearing a blue dress.

THE IMPERFECT CONTINUOUS TENSE

This is similar to the present continuous tense. See page 65 for notes on the formation of continuous tenses.
The imperfect continuous is used to describe something which was happening in the past but which has now finished:

e.g.   estaba jugando al tenis con sus amigos - he was playing tennis with his friends.

THE CONDITIONAL TENSE   See page 37

THE FUTURE TENSE   See pages 27 and 28

PRESENT PARTICIPLES   See page 65 for formation

THE SUBJUNCTIVE

FORMATION

An easy way to remember this is that the verb endings change to behave like their opposites; -AR verbs adopt -ER verb endings and vice versa, apart from the first person singular.

Comprar	Comer	Vivir
compre	coma	viva
compres	comas	vivas
compre	coma	viva
compremos	comamos	vivamos
compréis	comáis	viváis
compren	coman	vivan

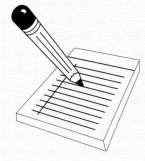

Radical changing verbs follow their usual pattern for changes.
Note the following irregular verbs:

estar	–	esté
dar	–	dé
saber	–	sepa
ser	–	sea
ir	–	vaya

It is used in the following circumstances:

a) After expressions of wanting or preferring, when the subject of the sentence changes:

e.g. quiero que <u>sepas</u> - I want <u>you</u> to know.

b) After verbs which express emotions such as joy, sadness, fear, anger, hope etc.

e.g. espero que <u>tengas</u> suerte en tus examenes - I hope that you are lucky in your exams.

c) After verbs of commanding or instructing:

e.g. mi padre dice que no <u>vaya</u> - my father says that I can't go.

d) After a negative or indefinite sentence (i.e. about an unknown person):

e.g. no conozco a nadie que <u>sepa</u> - I don't know anyone who knows.

e) After expressions implying doubt or improbability:

e.g. dudo que <u>esté</u> enfermo - I doubt that he is ill.

f) After certain conjunctions referring to future time, for example 'cuando', 'en cuanto', 'después de que':

e.g. cuando <u>tengas</u> diecisiete años - when you are 17.

g) After certain expressions:

es mejor que	–	it is best that
es necesario que	–	it is necessary that
es posible que	–	it is possible that
es imposible que	–	it is impossible that
es probable que	–	it is probable that
sin que	–	without
aunque	–	although
quizás	–	perhaps
tal vez	–	maybe

| PERSONAL 'A' | See page 63. |

| POR **AND** PARA | See page 51. |

| NEGATIVES | See page 23. |

PREPOSITIONS

Prepositions indicate where a person or an object is.

e.g.   en - in, on, by
en la mesa - on the table.

Many prepositions are followed by 'de':

e.g.   enfrente de - opposite,   al lado de - next to.

Remember that if the next word is masculine singular you will need to shorten 'de el' to 'del':

e.g.   al lado del cine - next to the cinema.

Some prepositions can be used with an infinitive to mean ...ing:

e.g.   antes de comer - before eating
al llegar - upon arriving
en vez de dormir - instead of sleeping

PRONOUNS

Pronouns are words which substitute nouns in order to avoid repetition. See page 17 for subject pronouns.

| DIRECT OBJECT PRONOUNS | See page 35. |

INDIRECT OBJECT PRONOUNS

See page 49.

Note that 'gustar' and 'doler' both require an indirect object pronoun:

e.g.   me gusta la sangría - I like sangria
le duele la espalda - his back hurts

POSITION

Indirect object pronouns usually go <u>before</u> the verb.

However they can be attached to the end of an infinitive:

e.g.   voy a comerla más tarde - I'm going to eat it later.

Or to the end of the present participle:

e.g.   estoy lavándome - I am washing (myself)

They come at the end of positive commands:

e.g.   déme el cuaderno - give me the book.

When a direct and indirect object pronoun come together then the indirect one comes first:

e.g.   démelo - give it to me.

POSSESSIVE PRONOUNS

These agree with the noun they are replacing.

Masculine singular	Feminine singular	Masculine plural	Feminine plural	English
mío	mía	míos	mías	Mine
tuyo	tuya	tuyos	tuyas	Yours
suyo	suya	suyos	suyas	His, hers, yours (formal)
nuestro	nuestra	nuestros	nuestras	Ours
vuestro	vuestra	vuestros	vuestras	Yours
suyo	suya	suyos	suyas	Theirs, yours (formal)

e.g. ¿Es tu mochila? Sí, es <u>mía.</u> - Is this your rucksack? Yes, it's <u>mine</u>.

If the possessive pronoun does not immediately follow the verb 'ser' it needs 'el/la/los/las' before it:
e.g. Tu hermano es más inteligente que <u>el mío</u>. - Your brother is more intelligent than <u>mine</u>.

DEMONSTRATIVE PRONOUNS   See page 47.

DISJUNCTIVE PRONOUNS

These are used after prepositions, e.g. para, cerca de, detrás de.

mí	-	me
ti	-	you
él/ella/usted	-	him/her/you (formal)
nosotros/as	-	us
vosotros/as	-	you
ellos/ellas/ustedes	-	them/you (formal)

e.g. Este regalo es para <u>ti</u>. - This present is for <u>you</u>.

Note: conmigo - with me
contigo - with you

RELATIVE PRONOUNS   See page 55.

Y AND O

Y means 'and' <u>but if</u> it is followed by 'i-' or 'hi-' then it changes to 'e';
e.g. Geografía <u>e</u> Historia. - Geography and history.

O means 'or' <u>but if</u> it is followed by 'o-' or 'ho-' then it changes to 'u';
e.g. Tiene siete <u>u</u> ocho gatos. - He has seven or eight cats.

NOTES

ROCK · LIVES
THE ULTIMATE STORY

THE ARTIST FORMERLY KNOWN AS
Prince

ROCK · LIVES

THE ULTIMATE STORY

THE ARTIST FORMERLY KNOWN AS

Prince

STEVEN ROSEN

Design: Slatter-Anderson
Printed through: World Print, Hong Kong
Cover photograph: Pictorial Press Ltd
Photographs: Neal Preston, Redferns, Pictorial Press Ltd

Published by Castle Communications plc, A29 Barwell Business Park, Leatherhead Road,
Chessington Surrey, KT9 2NY.

ISBN: 1 860740 456